T0314142

JUST HERE FOR THE COMMENTS

Lurking as Digital Literacy Practice

Gina Sipley

BRISTOL
UNIVERSITY
PRESS

First published in Great Britain in 2024 by

Bristol University Press
University of Bristol
1–9 Old Park Hill
Bristol
BS2 8BB
UK
t: +44 (0)117 374 6645
e: bup-info@bristol.ac.uk

Details of international sales and distribution partners are available at bristoluniversitypress.co.uk

British Library Cataloguing in Publication Data
A catalogue record for this book is available from the British Library

ISBN 978-1-5292-2727-7 hardcover
ISBN 978-1-5292-2728-4 paperback
ISBN 978-1-5292-2729-1 ePub
ISBN 978-1-5292-2730-7 ePdf

Cover design: Andy Ward
Front cover image: iStock / Ilona Shorokhova
Bristol University Press use environmentally responsible print partners.
Printed and bound in Great Britain by CPI Group (UK) Ltd, Croydon, CR0 4YY

FSC
www.fsc.org
MIX
Paper | Supporting
responsible forestry
FSC® C013604

For Tristan, Colin, and Emmet

Contents

List of Figures and Table

Figures

Table

About the Author

Gina Sipley is Associate Professor of English at the State University of New York at Nassau Community College and Affiliate Faculty in the Women's and Gender Studies Project. She currently serves as English Program Coordinator and Vice Chair of the Creative Writing Program. She has previously served as Coordinator for Emerging Educational Technologies and Director of the Stony Brook University Coding in the Schools Program. Her research about literacy, lurking, and emerging technologies has been published in *New Media + Society*, *Selected Papers of Internet Research* (AoIR), *Journal of Educational Technology Systems*, and presented at the Association of Internet Researchers, the Modern Language Association, and SXSW EDU conferences. She has written op-eds for *The London School of Economics Impact Blog*, *Al Jazeera America*, *EdSurge*, *Mic*, and *Newsday*. She is a first-generation college graduate.

Acknowledgements

On being a mother and being a writer, Ursula LeGuin declares 'the hand that rocks the cradle also writes the book'.

Parenthood should not limit our aspirations; however, what LeGuin does not illuminate is that the book can only be written if other hands are making dinners, doing laundry, and actively caring for the children. This book would not have been completed without access to excellent on-site affordable childcare provided by the teachers and caregivers at The Children's Greenhouse at the State University of New York (SUNY) at Nassau Community College under the direction of Janet Walsh. Alexandra Dunleavy, Martha Braun, and Karen Greene cared for my children during semester breaks when I was off-campus. Most importantly, Tristan Sipley, PhD, my magnificent other, took the household and parenting lead on many early mornings, late evenings, and weekends. His commitment to our family allows me to be the best version of myself. This collective support freed my hands to pick up the pen and write.

Paul Stevens has championed this project since we first met at the Association of Internet Researchers Conference. His dedication and guidance, alongside the fantastic team at Bristol University Press, including Georgina Bolwell, Bahar Celik Muller, Zoë Forbes, Alexandra Gregory, Ellen Mitchell, and Freya Trand, have brought this book to life. Dawn Preston and the team at Newgen Publishing provided excellent production and copyediting services. I am grateful to the anonymous reviewers of the book proposal and manuscript for generously giving their time to offer thoughtful and constructive feedback. There are many people who helped me to acquire important materials, read early drafts, think through the salient points, develop my writing, make revisions, and focus my attention: Collin Gifford Brooke, Joanne Bergbom, Rachel Collins, David Crugnola, William Davies, Michael Dwyer, Robin Edkin, Brigitte Fielder, Alan Flurkey, Deborah Fossett, Lynette Hammond Gerido, Mercer Hall, Anne Henrichs, Jeanne Henry, Sara Hosey, Elisha Lim, Dina Ledwith, Jeanette Liotta, Robert Liotta, Theresa McGinnis, Lori Miata, Andria Milone, Serena Mooney, Vicente Perez, Whitney Phillips, Rose Tirotta-Esposito, Jonathan Senchyne, Tiana Walters, and the pseudonymized participants who were interviewed for this book. The Nassau County Public Library System provided space for reflection, writing, and research, and I am particularly indebted to Michael Morea, Mary Birk, and Richard Brower at the Gold Coast Public Library. Laura Portwood-Stacer and the Manuscript Works Book Proposal Accelerator offered candid feedback on the manuscript and vital insights into the acquisitions process. The early stages of the research for this book were supported through funding I received while writing my dissertation. I wish to thank Hofstra University for their generous funding, SUNY Nassau Community College for granting me a full year sabbatical to complete my dissertation research, and to SUNY for providing funds through the Innovative Instruction Technology Grant for the Tools of Engagement Project (now known as the Emerging Technologies for Lifelong Learners Massive Open Online Course) to offset my academic fees.

Tristan, Colin, and Emmet Sipley offered days full of joy, humour, and love – the necessary fuel to complete this work. Without them, this book would not exist.

Introduction: Everyone's a Lurker

An autoethnographic confession: I'm a lurker

My mother-in-law was the first person to call me a lurker. I don't think she meant it as an insult per se, but to me, the word conjured images of an evil and calculating villain hiding in the shadows. Sure, I stopped using Facebook to post photos of my children, her grandchildren, and occasionally used it to scroll through my newsfeed, but was that really so bad?

From the beginning I have had an inconsistent approach to Facebook participation. I was a 22-year-old graduate student instructor in the early 2000s when I first became aware of the social media network, and I only learned about it because some undergraduates created a nasty Facebook group about one of my colleagues. Although my colleague was not active on Facebook, another instructor discovered the group while browsing the site and brought it to the attention of our supervisors to take disciplinary action. In those early days of Facebook, colleges did not have policies on appropriate student social media use. Bloggers and the local press debated what role, if any, the university should take in disciplining the students who had written vile comments about their instructor. It was the advent of social media reporting and the writers neglected to think through the ethics of mentioning this instructor's full name in their reports. Search engines indexed the story under the instructor's name, making public the lurid details of the students' writing, which had previously only been accessible to those on Facebook. Given the ludicrously competitive academic job market, this could be disastrous for anyone's career. When I joined Facebook that year, I did it solely to learn what, if anything, my own students were saying about me that could potentially derail my career. In hindsight, I joined the platform to lurk.

It took me a good two years or so to delurk, to become comfortable with the idea of posting photos or status updates, and even when I did, I kept it to a minimum.[1] Social media was just a casual way to keep in touch with friends as I moved around the country. However, every time I thought I had a sense of the rules and social norms of the site, they changed. Navigating the etiquette of Facebook became anxiety-inducing as my Facebook friends expanded to include seemingly everyone I had ever encountered in my life: from a University of Edinburgh student who let me sleep on the floor of her dorm room one night when I ran out of money while travelling, to a high school classmate who I remember only as the kid who got arrested for (accidentally) setting an American flag on fire after 9/11. In what alternate universe would I ever invite these two people to my house for dinner? At what event would they be guests, alongside my mother, my boss, and the priest from the Newman Centre at my college? And yet here we all were together sharing space on the internet. There seemed to be no message I could confidently pen that would be palatable to all audiences. Sure, lots of people have highly curated lists of friends, purging contacts who become offensive or meticulously crafting privacy circles to ensure barriers between disparate groups of friends. But that seemed like a lot of work for something that was just supposed to be a fun diversion. Unfriending felt rude, yet starting a conversation, even about the most banal of topics like birthdays, seemed to be a landmine. I was expected to either wish everyone I had ever met a happy birthday or to select which Facebook 'friends' were worthy of my cheer.[2] And would it be sufficient to merely type Happy Birthday, or did I need to create a photo collage and type a message alluding to inside jokes to truly show my love? Before social media I might add a note in cursive to the message already printed inside a birthday card to a select few friends as a way to demonstrate my fondness, but to others I would just quickly scrawl 'Love, Gina'. Birthdays on Facebook are a public display. Posting a loving tribute to my mother, which I know will be seen and read by friends who are estranged from their own mothers, seemed cruel. Not acknowledging my mother's birthday with a heartfelt message and photo collage makes me look cold-hearted.

Beyond the rather low-stakes decision of whether to wish someone a happy birthday, the thought of publicly commenting on political issues leaves me short of breath. The polite thing to do, for me, was to say nothing at all. But this wasn't good enough for Facebook. Mark Zuckerberg has famously said that 'having two identities for yourself is a lack of integrity',[3] but living in his world of context collapse, where there are no barriers between relationships, is exhausting.[4] Friends both left and right of centre would often memetically post the same picture quote of a citation attributed to Howard Zinn: You can't be neutral on a moving train.[5] They urged their fellow social media users to take a stand for their respective issues. I was doubtful that liking a pro-Palestine post would actually improve the lives of Palestinians, but I was certain it would involve a confrontation with some Zionist friends and it could also get me fired. At the time I was a middle and high school teacher at an independent school with few job protections and I really needed the income and flexible working hours from my job. I was petrified of inadvertently expanding my network to include my students, or worse the parents of my students, who might complain about something I wrote on social media to the headmaster or board of trustees. Privacy settings became more and more confusing to navigate, encouraging constant engagement. In response, I simply stopped adding friends. The more participation Facebook demanded from me, the less I wanted to give it and, by 2011, I was done posting.

But this did not mean I was done reading. Social media, Facebook in particular, is notoriously difficult to quit.[6] Even people who declare they are leaving Facebook are usually just taking a sabbatical for a few days or weeks to detox. I would still log on occasionally to check my newsfeed, and over time I noticed that many of my closest friends were also posting less and less.[7] Like me, though, they were also still reading. I knew this because occasionally I would get group text messages with a screenshot of a ridiculous post made by a mutual acquaintance. We would share an emoji-filled snicker that reminded me of passing notes in biology class, a private aside from the public performance of high school theatrics. When I became a homeowner, neighbourhood Facebook groups became a vital resource for everything from basic questions about septic system maintenance to the absurd: who to call if you found a vulture devouring a raccoon on your sidewalk. I developed a trove of local business resources to actively support and suggest to others. Most of my business referrals happened offline in real-world conversations at school drop-offs or at backyard barbecues among neighbours who were not posting in the groups either but seemed to read it with the same regularity that they did our local *Herald* community newspaper. When I would encounter the rare personal post from a distant friend or acquaintance who was struggling – with cancer, addiction, homelessness – I reached out, off-social media, to check in or to send a direct donation. In some cases, I did this to circumvent fees, so that the recipient could access a larger contribution, but mostly I wanted a way to more genuinely show my support. I didn't want to be just another comment in a thread.

My reasons for lurking seemed justifiable, so in response to my mother-in-law's comment, I laughed it off: I'm a lurker. Yes, I am.

And the research says: you're a lurker, too

But were my reasons really justifiable? This playful exchange with my mother-in-law got me thinking about the word lurker and whether or not it was an appropriate term to describe the phenomenon of being 'Just Here for the Comments' as many a meme shouts on a heated commenting thread. In a highly unusual career twist, I boomeranged back to academia to finish my PhD in literacy studies while on the tenure track at a community college and I decided to make lurkers and lurking the focus of my studies. My dissertation was a two-part qualitative study of 15 New York City suburban neighbourhood Facebook groups during the COVID-19 pandemic.

Utilizing a community mapping of 203 participants and extensive interviews with 18 group members, I set out to describe the literacy practices involved in lurking and to describe the Facebook features, policies, and transactions that may encourage lurker literacies. Beyond this dissertation dataset I have conducted 15 additional interviews about lurking as a literacy practice.

One of the many things my research reconfirmed is that lurking, or reading the comments in an online group without writing a comment, is a common practice.[8] In the early internet days, message boards had fewer users because online communities were smaller; internet access was a privilege. In 1983, 10 per cent of adults in the United States had a personal computer in their home, and of that group only 14 per cent used an internet modem, resulting in an estimated 1.4 per cent of US adults using the internet.[9] The year 1983 was also the year that the word lurker, as related to internet reading, appeared in print in the *New York Times*.[10] People who identify as (or were identified as) lurkers were a somewhat distinct group because internet users themselves were a small percentage of the population. As the internet has come to dominate all aspects of our lives, lurking has become a habitual practice for those with easy access to smartphones and Wi-Fi. There is simply too much content available to respond to everything. Moreover, even when the internet was limited to only those who could afford and understand how to set up a connection, a projected 90 per cent of all members in an online community group were lurkers. This initial informal 1998 study by Jon Katz on the tech news website *Slashdot*[11] has since been replicated at least six times by scholars studying participatory culture, most notably by researchers (Robert) Blair Nonnecke and Jenny Preece.[12] In each instance, the studies showed that the majority of the participants were lurking. Not only is lurking omnipresent, it is a context-specific choice. You might lurk on Facebook, but post heavily on LinkedIn. You might consider yourself active on X, formerly known as Twitter, because you post a lot under the #BlackLivesMatter, while also lurking on the #BlueLivesMatter. Our geography has an efferent impact on our choice of when to lurk.[13] If you are scrolling through Instagram while waiting on the subway platform and your train arrives, your attention is diverted; you are less likely to respond to something riveting. If you are leisurely sitting on the toilet watching TikToks, you might find the time to write a lengthy comment on something mundane. Thus lurking, when we choose to restrain rather than respond, is a continuous choice we make as we navigate across platforms.

In digital spaces lurkers are too often described, by both researchers and journalists, as greedy 'selfish free-riders' who take, but contribute nothing, to an online discussion. This thinking has its roots in early studies by Peter Kollock and Marc Smith.[14] Through this lens, contribution is seen as a social good that adds to the repository of collective knowledge or the hive mind. Anyone not contributing is viewed as a threat. Lurking is also seen as an anti-aesthetic response. Scholarship on participatory culture is closely linked to creator culture with emphasis on the tools, processes, and sociological impact of creating new digital texts. In a discussion with Henry Jenkins and Mizuko Itō on participatory culture, danah boyd questions the current emphasis on active participation as a more valuable contribution than passive participation. She asks, 'What does it mean to always focus on active participation, regardless of the quality of that contribution?' and posits these salient questions: 'Can someone be a valuable and participatory lurker?' and 'What does high quality listening look like?'.[15] From a literacy studies perspective, 'high quality listening', which includes looking at posts and links and thinking about them, is a metaphor for reading, and reading is a highly active process. Where boyd believes that it is possible for lurking to be a participatory act, Jenkins, in the context of this conversation, is hesitant to ascribe too much value to participation that does not leave a visible trace within the commenting field.[16] These types of discussions have a common corollary within print-based literacy studies in regard to annotation. Is the reading experience diminished when we do not annotate texts? Perhaps. But was that reading experience without value? If participation is contained within creator culture, does that mean that pre-internet readers in the mid-20th century and prior who read novels and then did not either publish a book review or write literature in response have a meaningless or inactive reading experience? Rethinking lurking as a literacy opens up a new way to ascribe value and make visible the participatory acts that carry across platforms and into real-world spaces when we read but do not comment.

Literacy practices of lurkers

What does it mean to be a lurker? Lurking is frequently defined in academic studies by the ratio of the number of messages sent by a user in relation to the total messages exchanged in the group.[17] These early studies provided a necessary preliminary step to call attention to the existence of lurkers and to illuminate the ordinariness of the practice. Demonstrating its commonality was an attempt to destigmatize it. To add to this foundation, *Just Here for the Comments* explores lurking within a sociocultural framework of situated literacies. Situated literacies refers to the idea that 'literacy is best understood as a set of social practices' and that these practices are both historical and evolve over time.[18] Literacy is more than decoding and reproducing because 'understanding literacy requires a third specification – its use in and application to precise, historically specific material and cultural contexts'.[19] This sociocultural framework is a response to earlier notions of education rooted in post-Enlightenment ideals which viewed literacy through an autonomous model of mastering reading and writing as technical and neutral skills. Viewing literacy as a plurality, rather than a binary distinction of literate or illiterate, allows us to study microscopic dimensions of power. In essence, literacy practices are what people do with literacy. They are not static; rather new practices continue to develop in response to social and cultural phenomena. Lurking is one such evolution of the literacies that have emerged from the invention of computing and digital technologies.

Within digital and media literacy studies, the word literacy is too often used metaphorically for technological skill development or as a limited means to assess one's ability to identify media bias or disinformation.[20] By theorizing the role of the lurker, I recentre the discussion on literacy as a reading practice by applying print-based reading research and frameworks to social media use. In her 2018 SXSW EDU keynote, danah boyd questioned the efficacy of the current state of media literacy and she was, at that time, a dissenting voice.[21]

What we read on social media regularly influences the fate of elections and can undermine our democracy.[22] The storming of the US Capitol by an autogolpe organized on the now defunct social media app Parler, whose groundswell of support was dependent upon lurkers alongside those leading the charge in commenting threads, illuminates one example of the necessity of understanding how readers make meaning and take action based on their interpretations.[23] Moreover it is understood within literacy studies that literacy practices need not be commodified to exist. The advent of social media, particularly its front-facing system of vanity or publicity metrics, provides an immediate illustration of some, but not all, of the digital literacy practices that exist. Objects of publicity metrics generally include comments, likes, shares, emoji reactions and other more platform-specific gestures that publicly measure interaction. These objects can be used to ascribe social influence within a platform or be corroborated with metrics from across social networking sites to create an influence and impact score. The data produced by lurking, or reading without engaging in publicity metrics, cannot be easily observed by other social media users. Companies that provide social media services have access to hover metrics and micro-metrics, which track minute interactions like click-response rate to impressions, but researchers are often locked out of this proprietary back-end data. Even those at social media companies with access to hover and micro-metrics data lack the full context of the reader's comprehension and application of the ideas encountered. Therefore, lurker literacies can best be visualized through qualitative research methods.

Lurking is a heterogeneous literacy practice. During the interviews conducted while writing this book, participants describe a variety of reasons for lurking and styles of lurking they engaged in in response to the content they read. In this book I explore five lurker literacies that demonstrate valuable and participatory acts. Since my research centred on the American social media experience, future studies of lurkers and lurking on a global scale are necessary to identify a wider range of lurker literacies. My compilation of lurker literacies is not meant to be exhaustive, but rather lays the foundation for subsequent work on the evolution of the literacy practices of lurkers. These lurker literacies will be discussed in greater depth in the coming chapters.

In an effort to illustrate the subtleties of the impact of lurking, each of the six body chapters open or close with an analysis of a meme. By dissecting the image text and locating the source context for the image, I use these memes as a frame through which to discuss how lurker literacies operate. Many of the chapter titles allude to popular lurker memes. Chapter 1, '"Don't Mind Me": The History of Lurkers from Lerkere to *Thriller*', historicizes the myth of the lurker, tracing its roots from real-world abuser to surreptitious online reader by contextualizing a range of cultural texts from 14th-century poems to 21st-century memes. Lurking is perceived as malignant when its motives resist anthropocentrism, imperialism, and capitalism. This chapter sets out to problematize the negative connotations of lurking and illuminates the ways that lurking can be an active, participatory, and valuable act. Chapter 1 introduces reflexive entertainment as a lurker literacy. Reflexive entertainment is when a reader chooses to leisurely browse through social media platform content for distraction and amusement, but while doing so encounters salacious content that disrupts their flow. Encountering this antagonistic or bullying content makes the reader question their own morals and ethics. One engages in identity negotiation in relation to what they have read, making a decision about whether or not they want to delurk, desist, or defend. Delurking can take the form of either bullying or defending the target in the commenting thread. Among those who choose to remain lurking, there are two paths forward. One is to desist, a practice where the reader will stop reading the post because they do not want their presence to contribute to the laughter. The other is to continue to read and avoid publicity metrics engagement in favour of using offline defence methods to support the target. Having established in Chapter 1 that internet lurking is a participatory heterogeneous practice, Chapter 2, 'Readers Have History: Towards a Transactional Theory of New Literacies', explores the relevance of transactional and sociocultural print-based literacy theories to the digital reading experience. At the centre of this discussion is an illustration of the shifting notions of author and reader on social media and how theories of print-based literacy are necessary for understanding the efferent and aesthetic motives of readers, which includes the decision of when to engage in specific lurker literacies.

Chapters 3 and 4 introduce community mapping and interview data to explore the literacy practices used while lurking and the gratifications sought by lurking. Utilizing data from neighbourhood Facebook groups, Chapter 3, '"To Let Others Know They Are Not Alone": Lurking and Community', analyses the ways that offline relationships influence online behaviour. This chapter argues that receptive reading, protective curation, and participatory restraint are lurker literacies readers engage in on social media to gratify desires to preserve their offline relationships with members of their community. Receptive reading occurs when a person wants to closely, and anonymously, read a social media commenting thread with the express purpose of understanding a divergent point of view. Protective curation is when a person reads to collect information to protect their socioeconomic status. This includes gathering information to professionally advance in one's career and/or to maintain the perceived quality of their community life. Participatory restraint is a strategic choice whereby a person will purposefully not respond to an inflammatory social media post because they want to limit the 'oxygen of amplification' and contain the story.[24] These efforts are sometimes taken individually and are sometimes collectively decided by a group using alternate, non-social media, communication methods. A reader will purposefully refrain from commenting, liking, or sharing their dissent via publicity metrics. Chapter 4, ' "Aint That Special": Moderating in the Age of Digital Exploitation', explores the unpaid digital labour of moderators and how moderation style encourages or discourages a reader's visible participation. This chapter examines three specific case studies – affinity groups (online communities where members share in a common goal), health communities, and neighbourhood groups – and introduces sensemaking to the discussion of lurker literacies. The chapter also offers critical content analysis of the evolution of Facebook group features and the corporation's community management training programme to offer insights into the challenges of active Facebook moderation. Facebook's moderator model is contrasted with the absence of moderators on X, formerly known as Twitter, which operates on a binary structure of followers/following. The latter creates an environment where lurking is an assumed central, rather than peripheral, practice.

Ignoring lurkers can invalidate critical social science research in education, health, and psychology, which often use social media participation as part of their data collection methods. If data collection does not account for lurkers, researchers reach only 10 per cent of social media users within the confines of their study. This could compromise the validity of the results and findings, thus having a detrimental effect on health and learning outcomes for people whose care and education rely on practitioners accessing accurate data. Thus, Chapters 5 and 6 delve into the real-world consequences of lurking. Chapter 5, 'Resistance and Refusal: (Re)Evaluating Media Literacy', argues that the internet is a colonized space and, within it, lurking is a privileged participatory act. Global media literacy standards are centred on acts of public participation and must adopt a more inclusive approach. Building on the work of media literacy scholars, this chapter seeks to broaden media literacy assessment from skill development and identifying bias to include the teaching of lurker literacies as resistance to surveillance and the amplification of misinformation. Finally, Chapter 6, 'How Do We Account for Lurking? Implications for Social Science Researchers', offers concrete strategies for ways to expand datasets to include the literacy practices of lurkers. It also explores the limits of platform sponsored tools like CrowdTangle for data collection and offers suggestions for how to ethically engage with lurkers.

The book's conclusion, 'Participatory. And Valuable?', extends the interrogative from which these studies began. Can lurking be valuable if participation is not publicly (and easily) measurable? This chapter unpacks value as a social and economic construct and discusses the impact lurking has for platforms, companies, society, and ourselves. Rather than disband the use of the term lurker, I argue that understanding ourselves as lurkers offers the possibility of more sustainable community relationships on and offline.

1

"Don't Mind Me": The History of Lurkers from Lerkere to *Thriller*

The cover of James V. Smith's horror novel *The Lurker* contains the tagline 'When the lights go out, he's coming to get you'.[1] There are roughly 60 horror novels in the WorldCat database with the word lurker in the title and they represent our worst fears about what happens when someone watches us without our knowledge.[2] Lurkers are imagined to be violent, self-serving, sexually deviant, socially inept, and trollish. These are characteristics built and maintained by anthropocentric, imperialist, and corporate entities who benefit from this narrative. Since contemporary internet lurkers are ubiquitous, and it is an act that everyone engages in from time to time, then of course some lurkers are violent, sexually deviant, self-serving, socially inept, and trollish because these are characteristics that are dominant in some people. But this also means that lurkers can be peaceful, cooperative, and socially progressive. As Chimandra Ngozi Adichie explores in her TED Talk, 'The dangers of a single story', without experiencing a plurality of stories, we are left with one incomplete and dominant narrative.[3] Understanding the architecture of a narrative requires examining the stories upon which it is founded. This chapter seeks not to debunk the myths of the lurker, but rather to offer nuance and historical context to highlight the power structures from which these perceptions emerge. Looking back on the origins of the lurker helps us to understand when digital lurking is truly problematic and to whom. This chapter moves strategically through the shifting denotations and connotations of the word lurk as catalogued in the *Oxford English Dictionary*, offering rich historical and social context. It concludes by looking closely at our contemporary historic moment and diving deep into the phenomenon of reflexive entertainment.

The hunter and the hunted

In casual speech and writing, lurking is a word that connotes the anticipation of a violence, the villain who is watching, waiting quietly to attack its prey.

The animal lurker in medieval literature is foremost an observer, without a premeditated wicked or immoral purpose. In the *Reliquiæ Antiquæ*, a collection of Middle English poems recorded in 1325, 'The names of the hare' contains the first printed use of lurker.[4] In this poem, the speaker lists 77 names for the hare as a lyric praise for the animal. The poem is imagined as a ritual a hunter would make upon encountering a hare. Although hares later come to have allegorical significance as tricksters, this does not occur until the 16th century. In the 14th century they are depicted as one close to god, a bearer of fertility, who unfortunately might need to be killed for sustenance. Through the praising recitation of names, the hunter hopes to lure the hare. It is not the hunter who is depicted as the lurker, however, but the hare itself. Among those 77 qualities of hare listed is that of the lurker, 'The wilde der, the lepere, The shorte der, the lerkere'. Reading Seamus Heaney's 1982 translation of this poem to modern English it becomes clear that the hunter is commending the contrasting size of the hare from when it is at its largest leaping ('lepere') with its shortest ('shorte') as a lurker ('lerkere').[5] In modern English, animals are sometimes described as lurking for their prey, but in neither a Middle nor modern English context, would this be an accurate depiction of hares. Since hares are herbivores, there is no need to lurk for dietary purposes. The praise given by the hunter is for the hare's ability to transform its size. In this first printed instance of lurker, the animal is a watcher who is regaled for its ability to shrink to its smallest, most diminished size.

The lurker appears again in 1399 in the anonymous alliterative verse poem 'Richard the Redeles'; this time taking the shape of a deceitful female partridge.[6] In the Old Testament Book of Jeremiah, those who enrich themselves by unjust means will be like the 'partridge that gathers a brood that she did not hatch'.[7] Proverbially, female partridges are deceptive; they will steal a mother's eggs through trickery and this duplicity will yield them no riches. The stolen brood will eventually leave for their natural mother. Playing on this proverb, 'Richard the Redeles' uses the partridge analogy as a way to critique the reign of England's Richard II and his usurper Henry VII. Lurker is not a term used in the Book of Jeremiah; it is one that the poet ascribes to its subject. In this allegory, Richard II is named the lurker, the false mother of England, and Henry VII is named the natural one who reclaims the throne. Attaching lurker to the unpopular King Richard II etches it into the English imagination as a slur, a way to describe someone who is deceptive and greedy.

It is important to remember that this text is a satirical poem whose purpose is to entertain. The text evokes a contorted biblical allusion that marks the shift in lurking from ambivalent watching towards fraudulent action. Later medieval writings, such as Nicholas Upton's *De Studio Militari*, explain that female partridges are treacherous because they pretend to be lame as a way to divert a hunter's attention away from their nesting offspring.[8] Again, the hunter in *De Studio Militari* is not described as lurking on the bird as its prey, but rather it is the female partridge who is the lurker by engaging in deception to protect her young. In an anthropocene sense she is a thief in the eyes of the hunter who seeks to accumulate the largest possible conquest, but this theft is not a violence on her part. The only potential violence that occurs is from the hunter who might kill her. This absence of violence is crucial to understanding how lurker evolves in the 19th century to encompass a creative thievery in resistance to capitalist gain.

Clever criminals

In 1842 an anonymous pamphlet began circulating in Birmingham, England titled *An Exposure of the Various Impositions Daily Practised by Vagrants of Every Description: Entered at Stationers Hall* and this is one of the first texts to describe lurking as a criminal pursuit.[9] The author collects data on vagrants, as a way to discourage giving alms to the poor, to defend the new Poor Laws, and to support England's workhouse system. The 1834 Poor Laws were devised as a way to reduce the cost of caring for England's poor through a nationalized system of workhouses. Public assistance in the form of housing and food would only be available if a person agreed to move into the workhouse where they were forced to wear a uniform and perform monotonous tasks and hard labour. The workhouse system was created as a way to save taxes for the British middle and upper classes; its purposefully harsh design intended to force those in poverty to find a job, any job, rather than seek assistance. One of the new kinds of vagrants that emerge in response is the lurker.

The lurker is considered to be the most financially successful of all the vagrants detailed in the pamphlet. They are defined as 'persons who go about with, briefs containing false statements of losses by fire, shipwrecks, accidents, etc. The seal and signature of two or more magistrates are affixed to them, and they are so well written'.[10] Catalogued in the pamphlet are examples of the kinds of lurks, the fraud that the vagrants engage in, to obtain donations. These include 'Fire-lurker', 'Shipwreck lurk', 'Foreigner's lurk', schemes where the lurker pretends to have encountered a catastrophe that reasonably explains their poverty and encourages the sympathy of prospective donors. In many of these examples, the lurkers are impoverished women, addicted to alcohol, who commit acts of deception – 'the sick lurk', 'the pregnant lurk' – to acquire money, food, clothes, or a place to rest.

The Edinburgh Review critiqued the pamphlet shortly after its dissemination to offer context for who the lurkers might be.[11] The journal goes to great lengths to document the rise in rural transient poverty due to the decrease in agrarian wages, and the rise of Irish immigrants fleeing the potato famine. Despite acknowledging the difficult conditions that have led to the increase in vagabonds, the article concludes with support for both the new Poor Laws and the workhouse system. By imagining no alternative to workhouses, *The Edinburgh Review*, a publication with wide distribution among the learned upper classes, reinforces the idea that lurkers are a subset of beggars who are slothful and refuse to work.

Around the same time, journalist Henry Mahew begins to observe and to interview working-class and impoverished people in London. Victorian London was one of the richest cities in the world and yet a significant portion of its residents were struggling to survive destitution. His articles for the *Morning Chronicle* illustrate, in meticulous detail, the trades in which working-class Londoners engaged, both legal and illegal, as well as their domestic lives. To complement these narratives, Mahew collected census-style details on the thousands of people living in these desperate conditions. His articles are later collected into *Labour and the London Poor*, four comprehensive book volumes that, unlike the Birmingham pamphlet on vagrancy, had and continue to have global readership. It is in what is later compiled as volume 1 that Mahew details the lurkers, a type of 'patterer', a thief who uses their voice to engage in deception.[12]

To be a lurker in 19th-century England required a sophisticated skillset: strong writing, reading, and speaking skills – what we refer to in the 21st century as literacy. The lurkers described in the pamphlet on vagrancy and in Mahew's *Labour and the London Poor* are not simply thieves, they are a specific class of White thieves who are actively participating in elaborate schemes and ruses to enrich themselves. Lurkers are considered more educated and skilled than the 'costers' with whom they are contrasted. 'Costers' are thieves described by Mahew as 'savage, primitive, brutish, Bedouins of the desert, Red Indian, Bosjesman, Carib, or Thug', who engage in 'darker pursuits'. The 'costers' will use violence as a means to securing their loot. In this caste of thieves, lurkers are viewed as the aristocracy. One of Mayhew's sources even claims that lurkers can make no less than £6,000 per year. Of course, this number seems to be hyperbolic, given that this sum would be higher than the yearly allowance of some nobility in 19th-century England, but the spirit of the statement is that lurking can provide liveable 'wages'.

The initial audience for both the Birmingham pamphlet and *Labour and the London Poor* were the British elite who were estranged from the living conditions of their neighbours. As readers, some developed sympathy they put into action to improve the conditions of the poor; others read to reinforce their contempt; and some read to be entertained by a class of people they hardly knew existed. Of these two works, Mahew's writings continue to have both scholarly and commercial appeal and have rarely been out of print in the almost two hundred years since they were first published. Mahew has come to be seen as not just a journalist, but as a social scientist: his text a crucial piece for historians and literary scholars as well as sociologists studying the lasting effects of poverty. Where his initial audience might not question lurkers as social deviants, contemporary readers have the privilege of distance and almost two centuries of scholastic research on the British class system.

Thievery in Victorian London is both an effect of poverty and a threat to the enterprise of the guardians, the local businessmen who operated the workhouses. Paupers interned in the workhouse endured horrid working and living conditions. In the Andover workhouse, for example, the master diverted funds for his own private gain by lowering the food rationings for inmates to the point of starvation. The physical, sexual, and psychological abuse guardians allowed workhouse masters to administer to the people indentured in their workhouses led Charles Dickens to write that in comparison to prisons, 'the dishonest felon is, in respect of cleanliness, order, diet, and accommodation, better provided for, and taken care of, than the honest pauper'.[13] Those who choose to lurk in Victorian England, when the choice is between succumbing to poverty or engaging in criminal action, do so because the spectre of prison is less dreadful than that of the workhouse. This linguistic turn towards lurkers as deviant continues to persist into the 20th century when lurking is reborn for the digital age.

Perverted readers

Where the lurkers of the late 19th century were criminalized, the lurkers of the late 20th century were sexualized because cyberspace was initially understood as an erotic zone. The term cyberspace was coined in William Gibson's 1986 science fiction short story, 'Burning chrome', where neuroelectronics enable sex workers at the upscale brothel, the House of Blue Lights, to be unconscious and unaware during the sex acts they perform.[14] The customers choose this particular brothel because it is a cyberspace where one can be both alone and with someone at the same time. Our nonfiction internet has provided this amorphous space to be together and yet apart for its users, a space that in tech reporting from the 1980s and 1990s was figuratively described in heteronormative sexual terms. Reporting on lurking was discussed within this metaphoric trope.

Digital lurkers first become known to the layperson in 1983 when Robert Lindsey's *New York Times* story, 'Computers as letterbox, singles bar and seminar', described a new personal computing technology – electronic bulletin boards – in which anonymous users began to meet and interact in early internet spaces like CompuServe.[15] Lindsey reports that 'some computer owners ... observe others' conversations, eavesdropping but not participating. Sometimes they even type lurking, so you know they are there'.[16] Thereafter, lurking became a term more commonly associated with computer behaviour.

By 1984 the perceived threat of lurkers was seen by corporations as an opportunity to market new products and services, specifically in response to sexual deviance. CompuServe runs a magazine ad for its CB Simulator that features a scrambler to allow users a private space to exchange information away from lurkers.[17] Lurking takes on a subtly sexualized connotation in this ad which features a nerdy curly brown-haired bride with oversized glasses at a computer keyboard, facing the magazine reader with the same gaze reserved for her digital paramour behind the computer screen. The bride is identified by her screen name, 'Digital Fox', in the advertisement's headline 'Thanks to CompuServe's CB Simulator, "Digital Fox" accessed "DataHari" and proceeded to an "Altared" state'. Digital Fox sits beside her mother who crouches down in her mother-of-the-bride gown to look into the glass of the computer screen, rather than a mirror; the portrait is cropped in the shape of a computer monitor.

The groom, 'DataHari', is an allusion to the Sanskrit God Hari who takes away all darkness and illusion, but yet in these early days of computing there are no photographs, videos, or images to be exchanged. This is a marriage solely of words: vows privately exchanged via the electronic bulletin board and any consummation limited to what can be expressed in print. One of the promises of the early internet was the possibility of privately finding community, maybe even romance, among like-minded souls. But privacy on the internet has always been an illusion. In the body text of the advertisement, CompuServe explicitly names 'lurkers' who 'get their kicks by watching' as a threat that could be remedied by purchasing a CB Simulator for its scrambler function. CompuServe also offers a 'private talk mode for guaranteed one on one conversation'. The implied reason for such privacy in this instance is as protection for the digital honeymoon. Cybersex was not yet an explicit discussion in popular culture, but those early internet users were aware of its existence.

Cybersex and explicit discussion of lurkers as sexual deviants reaches a wider audience in Charles McGrath's 1996 *New York Times* article, 'The internet's', that attempts to review all of the ways that users read the internet in an effort to give a review of the internet in its entirety.[18] He devotes a few paragraphs to cybersex meeting spaces like the CyberCity Hotel and Bianca's Smut Shack. He explains to readers unfamiliar with the term that these virtual sites are where users go to write and read pornographic texts, presumably while masturbating at their keyboard. He writes: 'If you're a "lurker", as those who prefer to watch, but not join in are known, the spectacle of all of this transparent loneliness and longing, of all this second rate, second-hand fantasy life is more than a little depressing.'[19] This is the only section of his comprehensive article where acting as a reader is described as lurking. Presumably it is because in these cybersex spaces masturbation is an act assumed to accompany reading and writing. Speculating on who the cybersex participants are, he writes: 'To judge from what they say about themselves, they're college kids, lonely housewives, bored office workers (a lot of computer sex seems to happen on company time).'[20] Unless McGrath counts himself among those bored office workers, he is someone reading within the group without exchanging messages or 'fully participating'; he is a lurker. However, not joining in doesn't mean that he is without contribution. He is reading the boards and then writing about them – for the *New York Times* audience rather than for the guests at the CyberCity Hotel. To come out as a lurker in the late 20th century would be to identify as a pervert.

In the 20th century the term pervert, as it is applied to abnormal or unacceptable sexual behaviour, was also too often attached to those with a desire for non-heterosexual relations. Lurking in cybersex spaces was an important part of sexual exploration, identity formation, and access to critical sexual health information for LGBTQIA+ people. As Michael Ross explains in 'Typing, doing, and being: Sexuality and the internet', the internet afforded an opportunity for coming out sexually that wasn't previously available, particularly to people living in rural communities.[21] Lurkers 'can watch the interactions, learn some of the language, and gain an understanding of what being gay is about'.[22] He describes two important stages for lurkers, observing and acculturating. In observing, lurkers understand at an 'earlier stage (or age)' whether or not what they are reading resonates with them and to what extent. In acculturating, they read to learn the 'language, culture, institutions, behaviors, attitudes, and beliefs' of gay life prior to sexual contact. The value of acculturation is that lurking provides a safer space that limits 'abuse, embarrassment, stigma, exposure, and violence'. Moreover, acculturation to the gay community in the 1990s has also been linked to lower levels of HIV infection.[23] The research linking lurking and LGBTQIA+ acculturation is a more recent study of past events. Early research on lurking was not ethnographic. It did not involve conversations with people about their habits or reasons for lurking. Rather it used a socioeconomic model to describe the value of lurkers within the limits of an online group. Although I am using the LGBTQIA+ community as but one example, the lack of early ethnographic studies of lurkers means that the perspectives of people who identify outside of White, upper-class and heteronormative positions are not accounted for.

Selfish free-riders

In the 1990s interdisciplinary scholars became interested in lurkers as, what they perceived to be, a perverse and homogeneously self-contained demographic. Researchers Peter Kollock and Marc Smith describe lurkers as 'selfish free-riders' in their 1996 chapter on 'Cooperation and conflict in online communities'.[24] They believe lurking is infectious. In their words, 'whenever one person cannot be excluded from the benefits that others provide, each person is motivated not to contribute to the joint effort, but to free-ride on the efforts of others'.[25] Online communities, in their view, are valuable if they are productive, and if they produce 'useful' content or artefacts. These community creations should only be available to those who actively and visibly contributed to their development. In essence, free-riding is theft. In their view, this free-riding will lead to a digital anarchy that empowers bad actors, trolls, and abusers.

In the same year, researchers Merrill Morris and Christine Ogan published a journal article, 'The internet as mass medium', where they reference free-riders as a threat to the critical mass necessary to sustain communication via online bulletin boards, Listservs, Usenet, and other online groups.[26] These online groups are a discretionary database[27] whose existence relies on a critical mass of at least 100 participants. Morris and Ogan also define the data within these databases, the conversations and the knowledge shared, as 'a public good'. In their view, contributing to this public good can only be achieved if participation is visible within the confines of the group. A similar discussion of lurkers as free-riders is included in scholars Barry Wellman and Milena Gulia's 1999 book chapter 'Net-surfers don't ride alone: Virtual communities as communities', where they explain that lurking 'does not support the group (because it is not easily observed online)'.[28]

Interestingly, Wellman and Guilia's chapter is included in *Communities in Cyberspace*, a book edited by Kollock and Smith, and is the only chapter within the collection to make a brief and passing reference to lurking. Kollock references free-riders in his chapter on gift exchange, offering the analogy that internet free-riders are like citizens who do not pay taxes, yet benefit from the national defence system, a public good funded through taxpayer dollars. Without further empirical evidence Kollock asserts that the motivation to free-ride is rooted in either 'greed' or a 'concern with efficacy' based on the low return on investment of one's time. In each of these instances, lurkers and free-riders are not considered valuable or participatory actors, nor are they considered as individuals with a history, geography, or culture that influences their decision to lurk.

In the early 21st century, (Robert) Blair Nonnecke dedicated the early part of his career to understanding lurkers as individuals and to offering empirical evidence to refute Kollock and Smith. He writes in his dissertation that 'every one of us has either lurked, is lurking or will lurk in the future'.[29] Purposefully using the narrowest definition of lurking (one post or fewer per month), 81 per cent of his participants were lurking on a distribution Listserv.[30] Most importantly, Nonnecke's research asserts that participation can include actions not visible within the group. Nonnecke asserts that:

[L]urking is not free-riding, but a form of participation that is both acceptable and beneficial to online groups. Public posting is but one way in which an online group can benefit from its members. Members of a group are part of a large social milieu, and value derived from belonging to a group may have far-reaching consequences.[31]

From his initial research and the scholars who sought to replicate his studies, we now know that there are many documented reasons why people lurk. In the interviews from his dissertation, he determined that lurkers:

- work to understand the social norms of the groups they have joined;
- try not to add to the chaos and keep communication clear by not contributing duplicating, irrelevant, or inflammatory posts;
- are well connected and share what they have learned in their offline networks;
- side post what they have learned in the group in other digital spaces; and
- commit to staying in the group.[32]

The findings of a Lurker Survey developed by Nonnecke and Preece and Nonnecke et al, revealed that for 60 per cent of the 1,188 survey participants the primary reason for not posting was because the user's self-reported informational needs could be satisfied by reading what others had written.[33] Building on this work, Preece et al later used a survey accessed by over 1,000 MSN message board users to determine that the top five reasons why people lurk on that site are:

> [1] not needing to post; [2] needing to find out more about the group before participating; [3] thinking that they were being helpful by not posting; [4] not being able to make the software work (i.e., poor usability); and [5] not liking the group dynamics or finding that the community was a poor fit for them.[34]

Other studies that offer more context for why people lurk include several health-related studies that demonstrate that lurking in online health communities can be a means of emotional empowerment.[35] Within educational studies, researchers who study new language learners have noted that Facebook lurking is a situation-specific behaviour and an acceptable Facebook practice among language learners.[36] In spite of these collective efforts, there are still many studies that approach lurkers as a homogeneous and socially deviant group and this impacts how lurkers are viewed in the popular press.

Trollish antagonizers

'You remember Trolls – not the rude lurkers online writing nasty remarks, but those little toys with round tummies' begins a movie review of the animated 2016 DreamWorks film, *Trolls*.[37] This lede exemplifies the way that trolls and lurkers are often conflated in journalism and popular writing. It also resonates with Kollock and Smith's early scholarly research on lurkers, which purported that lurking would lead to malevolent participation. In her exhaustive ethnographic research on North American internet trolls, scholar Whitney Phillips defines trolling as a spectrum of anonymous online behaviours motivated by a desire for lulz, a term she describes as 'a kind of unsympathetic, unambiguous laughter'.[38] Where some trolls and lurkers perhaps share a desire for anonymity, trolls pursue online mischief in pursuit of either their own personal amusement or the laughter of a group. 'Trolls believe that nothing should be taken seriously, and therefore regard public displays of sentimentality, political conviction, and/or ideological rigidity as a call to trolling arms.'[39] Trolling behaviours are active and can be captured by publicity metrics, which makes the mischievous activities of trolling easy to amplify. The performative and potentially viral (in the sense of quickly spreading across the internet) nature of trolling behaviours makes it a distinctly different process from lurking behaviours, which are difficult to capture via publicity metrics. The reasons why one might troll or lurk are therefore not synonymous.

Lurking has become a leisurely pastime for trolls and non-trolls alike. Where trollish antagonizers might initially lurk before choosing their target, they eventually delurk to engage in lulz. In the cyberspace theatre, trolls are bullies and lurkers are bystanders. Some bystanders will delurk and engage in a defence strategy on behalf of the target that is visible in the commenting field to all users. Whereas other bystanding lurkers will choose to engage in offline defence strategies that are never fully visible to the entire group. And some bystanding lurkers will remain surreptitious readers who take no further action on behalf of the target. Understanding the interplay between bully, target, bystander, and defender in digital spaces can best be understood through the analysis of memetic responses on a discussion thread.

When lurking for reflexive entertainment, a reader is negotiating their identity in relation to the audience. In an American context those who lurk for reflexive entertainment are popcorn munchers, a nod to the various popcorn memes that proliferate on social media when readers move from lurking to visible participation. Popcorn is itself symbolically significant. Since the 1930s popcorn has remained a cheap and delicious eat that keeps butts in seats and eyes focused on the screen, a snack deliberately chosen by the American movie theatre industry for its valuable return on investment. 'Popcorn was (and remains) relatively cheap to buy in kernel form, so the profit-margin was still high for sellers, even if it sold for pennies.'[40] Scrolling through social media for entertainment on the commenting thread, as opposed to watching a movie as a Netflix subscriber or reading the satirical

'Shouts & Murmurs' locked behind *The New Yorker*'s paywall is a cheap, accessible, and delicious thrill.

The 'Shit, the comments already started? Sorry. 'Scuse me' is a meme that often appears somewhere between the inciting action and climax of dramatic dialogue on a commenting thread on a social media platform like Facebook. By beginning the first sentence with a vulgarity, those users who share or laugh at this meme identify with the impolite connotations of lurking. As a sentence that is at once interrogative and rhetorical, it underscores the anticipation of an audience for the original post via the commenting thread. In other words, this particular meme projects the views of someone who read the original post and anticipated that there would be dramatic dialogue to follow. There is an intention to read the assumed full length of comments as they emerge. The second line of the meme, which is typed in a larger font, serves to both mimic the sentences people utter when they are quickly moving up the aisle to take their seat at the movie theatre ('Sorry. 'Scuse me'), and to indicate that in the virtual theatre of comments, the person sharing the meme is self-identifying as a member of the audience. This is a pseudo apology. Much like the person who enters the theatre late knows that their actions can be perceived as impolite, they seek to mollify the other members of the audience by offering a modest verbal apology. When social media users choose to share this meme they are not lurking, because they are engaging in publicity metrics and leaving behind an artefact of their transaction. But they are also acting on the instinct that there is a mass of silent observers quietly munching their popcorn in other rows. The person sharing this meme seeks to distinguish themselves from those other popcorn munchers and by doing so is offering a half-hearted apology for reading the comments for entertainment. For someone engaging in the lurker literacy of reflexive entertainment, encountering that meme is like the moment in a theatrical production where the actors break the fourth wall to acknowledge the audience.

Antagonism is visible in the most popular of the popcorn memes, the ones that allude to the movie theatre scene in the music video for Michael Jackson's *Thriller*. There are numerous versions of this meme, but the version that I am analysing is the one that was referenced most frequently in my interviews of Facebook group participants. This meme consists of a screenshot from the movie theatre scene in Michael Jackson's music video *Thriller* and two lines of text. The top of the meme in larger font states the phrase 'Don't mind me'. The bottom of the meme, in smaller font, asserts 'Just here to read the comments'. The choice to enlarge 'Don't mind me' is significant because it is a hypocritical phrase that purposefully and playfully calls attention to, first, the person who posts the meme; second, the original post; and, third, the full thread of comments. Any time a user posts a comment on a thread, it registers as a publicity metric that amplifies the reach of the original post and the commenting thread. Even if the user posts no original words, the very act of sharing a meme will enhance the value Facebook ascribes to the original post and its comments, and thus the original post and its comments will appear in the feeds of more Facebook users, likely those who are within the network of the original poster and everyone who has engaged in vanity metrics on the thread. By beginning with the word 'Just', the second, smaller, declarative sentence has an implied subject and predicate. The erasure of the words 'I am' removes personal accountability. To engage in ambivalent performative activity, particularly to get a laugh from the audience, is trolling, not lurking.

When these words are read against the *Thriller* screenshot image, the overall theme is much more sinister than that of the 'Shit, the comments already started?' meme. The screenshot image from *Thriller* shows a moment from the music video in the scene where it is revealed to the viewer that *Thriller* is an embedded narrative, or a story within a story. The inner narrative is an imagined 1950s nostalgia where two teenagers performed by Orla Ray and Michael Jackson are in a convertible car on a date that goes awry when the boyfriend reveals himself to be a werewolf. The outer narrative is a modern, 1980s teenage couple on a date in a movie theatre. They are watching a horror film, which happens to be the video footage of the 1950s couple from the inner narrative. Ray and Jackson also perform the role of the 1980s couple. The screenshot for the meme is a moment from the scene where it is revealed to the music video's audience that *Thriller* is a story within a story and that the outer narrative is cast as a realistic story in contrast to the fictional inner narrative. In that moment of realization for the viewer of the music video, Jackson is the 1980s boyfriend, gleefully eating popcorn. But his spectatorship is not benign. The ultimate twist to the music video is that the outer realistic narrative proves not to be a rational world. In the final scene of the music video, the 1980s boyfriend reveals to the music video audience that he, too, is a werewolf.

The scene on the 1980s movie screen that has piqued Jackson's character's attention is the boyfriend-turned-werewolf hovering over the screaming girlfriend in a manner that invokes the image of rape. It is not a fair fight between two equally weighted parties like one might watch in a boxing or wrestling match. It is a devouring of a vulnerable person by a more powerful creature. This is further complicated by the mise-en-abyme that Jackson is in essence watching himself. Mise-en-abyme, which roughly translates from the French to being caught in the abyss, is a way to describe the character's attention. The Droste effect of the film, 'where a picture appears recursively within itself',[41] has captured the boyfriend's attention, dragging him from the site-specific realities of the theatre down a narcissistic hole of unfathomable length.

What the meme decontextualizes is the shift in cinematic gaze from the 1950s date to the 1980s date. The meme focuses on Michael Jackson's face, but Michael Jackson is not alone in the theatre. In the music video, the cutaway scene from the 1950s attack is a full audience inside a movie theatre. The audience is captivated by the film. The faces of the audience show a range of expressions from shock, to fear, to gloom, but the only one smiling is Jackson's character. Styled in a signature red jacket, his bright white teeth beam in contrast to the darkness of the theatre and his own skin. He is cast in the centre of the frame of the music video and the viewer's eyes are set upon his laughter.

This is in sharp contrast to the next scene, three seconds later, which frames the 1980s couple. The girlfriend stares in horror at the film. She turns her body inward to her boyfriend, while the boyfriend does not shift his posture to comfort her. Ray's character asks, 'Can we leave?' and Jackson's character replies, 'Nooo. I'm enjoying it.' Jackson's character is enraptured with the scene of himself, and ambivalent to the emotions of those in the room of the movie theatre, including Ray.

This is emblematic of the horror of the embedded narrative of social media, particularly, Facebook posts. The inner layer of the embedded narrative is digital; it is the original post and those responding in the comments. The outer layer is the offline world of the reader's response as they lurk. When someone lurking encounters this meme it is a Lacanian moment of mirror stage, where the reader has caught a glance of one's self. In an essay titled 'The mirror stage as formative of the function of the I as revealed in psychoanalytic experience' in *Ecrits*, Lacan explains that within the 6–18 months of infancy a child 'playfully experiences the relationship between the movements made in the image and the reflected environment [of the mirror] and between this virtual complex and the reality it duplicates'.[42] This is a moment that demarcates the transition from pre-linguistic to symbolic order where one begins to understand their position in relation to others.

Lacan's psychoanalytic approach, read through the lens of continental philosophy and applied to cultural texts, can be understood as a moment where choice becomes obvious. Thinking through Lacan, lurking for reflexive entertainment is a literacy where the reader must decide whether to: (a) continue as a bystander and lurk down a commenting hole of unfathomable length; (b) delurk to engage in trollish behaviour and join in the blood-letting; (c) delurk as a defender to disrupt the devouring; or after catching a glimpse of one's self in an unflattering light; and (d) desist by leaving the post and/or closing out of the platform. The outermost narrative is an external conflict between Facebook and its user. Whether the user continues to lurk or to engage in vanity metrics, regardless of whether it is to stand up to the bully or to join them in their attack, the Meta corporation still profits from each and every interaction. Where lurking is a reading process that Facebook collects data on via hover metrics and impressions, it is not public-facing data.

Therefore, it is easy to forget that another real-world antagonist the reader is faced with is the corporation itself. Returning to the origins of lurking, we need to consider, who is the hunter and who is the prey in this new era of leisurely lurking? To what degree are our actions, as lurkers, really the problem? By engaging in reflexive entertainment, we can choose how we will respond to vicious social media content. Our personal choices are not always cruel. The outcome of reflexive entertainment can be benign, like the hare in the Middle English poem 'The names of the hare' or loving like the partridge in 'Richard the Redeles'. However, the corporation that funds the social media platform is like the boyfriend in *Thriller*, savoringly munching on the popcorn, while enjoying the savage exchanges. Whether, cruel, benign, or loving, each exchange increases the corporation's profitability.

★★★

The difficult-to-track, hard-to-commoditize nature of digital lurking is what makes it problematic for those who seek to monetize social media interaction. It is interesting to note that social media platforms are free of monetary cost for users because the payment for operating costs is derived from a user's consent in the terms of service agreement to data collection and surveillance. Although selfish and greedy have been terms used to describe the behaviour of lurkers as individual internet users, lurking in this sense could more accurately describe the social media business model. There have been attempts to destigmatize lurking, by instead using terms like Legitimate Peripheral Participant and Non-Public Participant.[43] Where the desire to neutralize the term is understandable, it diverts attention from the power structures at play when we engage in digital communication. As will be further discussed in Chapter 3, since lurker literacies comprise various socially situated online and offline literacy events, a more effective framework for moving forward is not to avoid the term lurking, but rather to begin to engage with it within the context of literacy studies.

Readers Have History: Towards a Transactional Theory of New Literacies

'Me at 3am reading all 388 comments of two strangers arguing on Facebook' is a meme that captures both the relationship between reading and lurking and the interdisciplinary complications of studying lurking as a digital literacy practice. Like all memes, various versions of 'Me at 3am' circulate on the internet. The time and the number of comments in the title can vary, but the title always includes a post-midnight time and a hyperbolic number of comments. Beneath the title is a screenshot of a classical painting of a man reading. The version catalogued in dopl3r, verbub, and other meme reference sites,[1] contains a screenshot of the 19th-century Carl Schleicher painting titled *Der Bücherwurm*, which translates from German as 'The Bookworm'.[2] In the painting an elderly man peers through his wire-rimmed spectacles at a page from a book. This book is one of many stacked high in a pile before him. His right hand pulls the page of the top book closer to his face while his left hand grasps for another book adjacent to the pile. The second book is slightly ajar: his index finger and thumb clutch a section for quick reference. He is a man caught between two good books, perhaps reading them side by side to place them in conversation with one another. This is a meme that ignites a nasal snort or a chuckle because commenting threads – whether on Facebook, email, fan forums, or another social media platform – can be enthralling like a good book that is hard to put down even though it is late, we are tired, and our morning alarm is only a few hours away from chiming.

There are three central reasons why the 'Me at 3am' meme is significant and relevant to our understanding of lurking. Foremost, similar to 'Just here for the comments' and 'Shit, the comments already started?', the words lurk, lurking, or lurker are absent in the title. The study of lurking is interdisciplinary and as Chapter 1 explores, the term lurking can contain negative connotations despite the historical and social contexts that suggest its normalcy and ambivalence. The omission of the words lurk, lurking, or lurker reinforce the difficulty of naming the phenomenon of reading, but not making one's presence as a reader known through engagement with publicity metrics. This chapter will dive into a discussion of audience, expectations, and the interdisciplinary terms used in place of lurking.

The humour in 'Me at 3am' relies on imagery that centres literacy and makes reading a visible part of participatory culture. Too often in technology studies, particularly in studies of media literacy, references to literacy are metaphorical and divorced from research on the reading process. In this chapter, I will unpack the ways that literacy studies offer a framework for understanding why the literal study of reading is a necessary addition to current research on lurking, specifically understanding why lurking occurs and its social effects.

Lastly the subject of 'Me at 3am' appears as a nameless, generic White male reader not unlike the one Roland Barthes imagines in his oft-cited essay, 'The death of the author'.[3] We laugh at 'Me at 3am' because the anonymity of Schleicher's subject allows us the possibility to insert ourselves into the situation. However, as lurkers, as readers, our experiences are not homogeneous. Through the lens of the theory of transactional literacy, put forth by Louise Rosenblatt, our positionality to the text and our stance as a reader varies depending on a variety of socially situated factors that are constantly in flux.[4] No reader can ever be without history. It is from this position of a rounded and fully developed reader that this chapter presents a reimagined model of Rosenblatt's Efferent–Aesthetic Continuum that can be applied to understanding lurker literacies among other forms of participation.

The audience and the reader

Too often in academia our disciplines and fields of influence are segregated in ways that limit our ability to more broadly understand a phenomenon and this is certainly true when it comes to lurking. Media studies and literacy studies are academic fields that share overlapping research interests in digital literacy and participatory culture. In these critical explorations, an influential strand of media studies, most prominently exemplified by Henry Jenkins, turns its attention towards the audience, whereas literacy studies centres on the reader. This is perhaps the most important distinction between the way that media studies and literacy studies view participation and yet both positions offer salient perspectives on how to conceptualize lurking. To better understand lurking it is necessary to first establish the nuances of the audience and the reader. Audience is a collective noun; it acknowledges a group of individuals. Whereas the reader is a singular noun and emphasizes the individual. Networked communication provides the 'potential to participate'[5] and the networked audience has the ability to respond as a content producer as opposed to a broadcast audience who is primarily a content consumer.[6] Since the networked audience is a collective of individuals, conceptualizing the audience is about understanding how individuals in the collective relate to one another. The polemical positionality of participation is one of perceived visibility and void. The possibility to create content provides a demarcation that leads to descriptions of participation that are often binary: public and non-public; creators and consumers; central and peripheral; active and passive.[7] This demarcation among members of the audience is linked to one's decision whether to leave a participatory trace that is visible to all members of the group. Within this binary opposition, public/creator/central/active participation is limited to what can be expressed through front-end web development and non-public/consumer/peripheral/inactive participation, otherwise known as lurking, is reserved for what can be seen through back-end web development and asynchronous offline spaces. Therefore, comments and other site-specific reactions like upvotes/downvotes, favourites, emoji, shares, and so on, which can be seen by all members of the group, receive a disproportionate amount of attention, in both the academy and in popular discourse.

There are binary similarities in literacy studies between the role of writers (or authors) and readers. Much of the philosophical musings on this subject, which depict the positions of author and reader as fixed, are based in a print culture that pre-dates the digital turn. The writer and the author, prior to the rise of networked computing and the proliferation of social media publishing platforms, were somewhat interchangeable terms. For clarity, I am going to use the term author in reference to the pre-digital era and the term writer for the post-digital era.

The Organisation for Economic Co-operation and Development estimates that 12 per cent of the world population was considered literate in 1840 (the first year global data was available) and 21 per cent of the world's population was literate by 1900.[8] Of this literate population, the status of author was applied to a small group of people. The 19th century saw both the rise in prominence of the novel as a literary genre and a widening distribution of mass-market paperbacks in the English language.[9] This elevated the status of the author, who was revered not just for the quality of the works he (and to a lesser extent, she) created, but because of the access they commanded to the means of production. This includes the cost of writing materials, the time afforded to the labour of composing, and the social capital to distribute and market the final product. Moreover, the process of canonization, the metaphoric anointing of certain texts to be literary and possess a universal greatness that demands an unquestionable reverence from readers, secured the elite position of the author.

Of course, literate people engaged in all kinds of writing, from letters and diaries to note-taking, but it is only with a contemporary scholarly eye that we place value on those utterances. To write did not make one an author. Access to publication, followed by the select canonization determined by critics and scholars, created a culture where the author in the 19th and early 20th centuries was akin to celebrity. He was the locus of knowledge and the sole interpreter of his text's singular meaning. This positionality has societal reverberations. The author commanded power beyond that of their text; they possessed a social voice. They were invited and expected to comment on moral, cultural, and political ideas for their readers. The process of teaching someone to read and write was an act of deference to the author. This will be further discussed in Chapter 5; however, readers were taught to emulate the author's style and thought rather than assert an individual or divergent opinion.

The celebrated status of the author begins to unravel in the mid-20th century. The writings of Mikhail Bakhtin, Roland Barthes, and Michel Foucault, among others, question the fixed positionality of author and reader.[10] As early as the 1920s, Bakhtin described the printed literary text as dialogic: the characters within a printed literary text exist as independent subjects, not objects of the author.[11] The idea that a character could have agency begins to shift attention from the author to their reader. Bakhtin viewed this dialogism as an invitation to a reader to respond. This way of thinking opens up two important distinctions: first, it gives the reader agency to command their own independent thoughts; and, second, it establishes that authors implicitly demand an exchange with their readers, whether or not that was their intention when they set out to write. The second point is one embedded in our current discussion of social media and the role of lurkers. The dialogic nature of composition in social media does not require a reply, but visible participation is nevertheless expected.

Jay Bolter extends Bakhtin's premise of dialogism by situating the online participation of writers and readers within its historical context.[12] The early 20th century was still the height of print culture; there were limited venues for literate people to author a published response to something they read in a book or periodical. Those venues were closely monitored and gate-keeping limited who was afforded the opportunity to respond. Moreover, the speed of production was more slowly paced. These material constraints predetermined a small pool of potential respondents. Therefore, it was reasonable to expect that the readers who were among the elite members of the audience could and would publish a response to what they have read, whether in the form of commentary or a literary work.

In our current contemporary moment, the capacity to be a writer is commonplace. The United Nations Educational, Scientific and Cultural Organization (UNESCO) Institute for Statistics calculated the global adult literacy rate for adults at 86 per cent, and the global youth literacy rate at 91 per cent in 2016, the most recent year that data is available. For countries in Central Asia, Europe, North America and Oceania, UNESCO found the global adult literacy rate to be 98 per cent.[13] This increased literacy rate, coupled with the explosion of emerging digital technologies, have broadened the potential of the audience to participate in the publishing process. In digital communication where there are numerous venues to respond, and fewer restrictions on who can respond, the pool of potential responders and responses is enormous.

In a Bakhtinian sense, there is still a subconscious expectation in online communities and on social media that the text one has authored requires a response. Howard Rheingold describes online communities as 'social aggregations that emerge from the Net when enough people carry on those public discussions long enough, with sufficient human feeling, to form webs of personal relationships'.[14] It is within this web of human feeling that silent reading is considered offensive and thus cast as lurking even though the silent reader may be a registered member of the group. The rapid scale and immense magnitude of digital content creation that is possible within a networked audience means that the absence of an individual's visible participation is simultaneously easy to overlook and yet also glaringly noticeable. This paradox is why the term lurking continues to persist despite the attempts to utilize the more neutralized language of non-public/consumer/peripheral/ inactive. There is still a perceived rudeness about reading and not leaving a visible trace to other members of an online community and this is entangled with the negative and predatory connotations of lurking discussed in Chapter 1.

Reading as metaphor

One of the biggest hurdles to introducing literacy studies to the study of lurking is that within the field of media and communication studies, literacy is a term that is often used metaphorically. Lurking can be conceptualized as a way of reading that has emerged from the invention of computing technologies. Emerging technologies, both the ones in existence at the time of this book's printing and the ones that have yet to be produced, have the capacity to redefine how we communicate. As literacy scholars Ken Goodman and Peter Fries explain, the invention of the printing press in the 15th century is remarkable not because of the pages it produced, but 'because of the literacy it makes possible'.[15] In the six centuries that followed the advent of print culture, our understanding of what it means to be literate and what it means to read continue to evolve. The International Literacy Association (ILA) currently defines literacy as '[t]he ability to identify, understand, interpret, create, compute, and communicate using visual, audible, and digital materials across disciplines and in any context'. The ILA definition also includes this note about the metaphoric application of the term literacy: 'Over time, literacy has been applied to a wide range of activities and appears as computer literacy, math literacy, or dietary literacy; in such contexts, it refers to basic knowledge of, rather than to anything specific to reading and writing.' There are specific historical reasons for this omission of the word reading.

In the 1980s teaching about the media began to emerge within scholarly discourse as a legitimate pedagogical endeavour and Len Masterman's seminal texts, *Teaching with Television* and *Teaching the Media*, are published.[16] During this time television is considered something to be 'demonized or dismissed', so this movement towards analysis and critique of television media is itself revolutionary.[17] Masterman outlines '18 principles of media education' and it is important to note that the term literacy is not included among the descriptions of these 18 principles.[18] Masterman preferred the term education over literacy. Within his vision for this new discipline, the most salient point is that 'Media Education is a serious and significant endeavour. At stake in it is the empowerment of majorities and the strengthening of society's democratic structures'.[19] Masterman frames his theories by thinking through the work of Barthes, specifically Barthes' *Mythologies* where he analyses French culture (wrestling, cooking, advertisements for toys, and so on) in the same manner that was once reserved for interpreting canonical literature.[20] Barthes remains a 'Grandparent of Media Literacy', a term coined by media literacy scholar Renee Hobbs.[21] The scholarly analysis of film, television, social media, video games, and so on, is possible because of the initial work by Barthes, which ushered in the post-structuralist movement in critical theory. It is the post-structural movement within literary and cultural studies that today has normalized the practice of a text being read through a range of lenses (Marxist, feminist, psychoanalytic, and so on) within the academy without any one particular reading of the text holding a place of superiority. Multiple interpretations of a text are possible, and those interpretations need not coincide with the way the author intended the text to be read. The value of Barthes' work, as perceived by Masterman and Masterman's successors, is the expansion of content worthy of analysis and that this cultural content, like literature, can be read.

Barthes, however, has some narrow views on what it means to be a reader. His influential essay, 'The death of the author', is considered a central source in cultural studies for expanding the possible ways of reading a text. By shifting analysis away from authorial intention, the death of the author brings about 'the birth of the reader'.[22] The reader who is liberated from the author's intent is free to explore their own interpretation. But the reader Barthes describes is someone who is without 'history, biography, psychology; he is simply that *someone* who holds together in a single field all the traces by which the written text is constituted'.[23] Barthes' reader is a nameless, faceless, and generalized reader. In other words, where a psychoanalytic reading of a text is possible, the reader themself is not (or should not be) influenced by their own psychology when offering an interpretation. By extension, under this frame the effects of the historical and biographical experiences of a reader are voided. This means that for Barthes a reader who has lived experience on the periphery of the dominant culture should not allow those experiences to influence their interpretation. In Barthes' *S/Z*, he describes the reader as 'intransitive'.[24] Rosenblatt, in a critique of Barthes' concept of readerly and writerly texts as expressed in *S/Z*, explains that although at first glance it may appear that Barthes celebrates the reader, to Barthes the reader can only offer an interpretation of the text that 'some authority, tradition, teacher, or critic, decrees is acceptable'.[25] There are significant raced, classed, and gendered complications to this homogenized reader and, by extension, to how we view lurkers.

The digital reservoir

The mythological history-less reader of Barthes' imagination persists in the generic way that lurkers are described and studied in academic literature. In early internet studies, content creators and content consumers had fixed positions and a pyramid model was used to represent the 90 per cent of lurkers or non-public/consumer/peripheral/inactive participation with the 10 per cent of public/creator/central/active participation.[26] This design structure was part of an effort to understand how to get more people to be creators and active participants. Studies on lurking emphasized ways to encourage participants to delurk and become more actively involved in the group.[27] Lurkers were a numeric generalized category of participants. They were mostly understood within the aggregate and their specific historical, biographical, and psychological reasons for lurking were not considered.

When analysing the networked audience, lurking is now beginning to be studied as part of a continuum of participatory practice upon which a person can oscillate among various degrees of participation. One is never exclusively a lurker, but rather lurking is an action a person chooses to take during digital participation. When studying lurking within media studies, this continuum is often viewed through examining the degree to which lurking dominates the general behaviour of the audience. This is sometimes described as a way to assess the overall health of a group or online community. It is important to note that these descriptions of dominance are often from the dawn of networked communication and persist into the early days of Web 2.0. They do not yet account for the ways that the social media ecosystem has evolved to include platforms that offer clearly defined cloistered groups or communities (for example, Facebook groups, Discord communities) where membership numbers are publicly shown and the limits of the group are relatively well known in contrast to open broadcast platforms (Instagram,

TikTok, and X) where an individual follows or has followers in an open arena that could potentially be viewed on or off platform.

To this end Henry Jenkins et al's *Spreadable Media* posits that:

> seeing participation as a model with increasing levels of more intense engagement masks the degree to which all participants work together in an economy operating under some combination of market and nonmarket logic, with various audiences performing tasks that support one another. From this perspective, a 'lurker' provides value to people sharing commentary or producing multimedia content by expanding the audience and potentially motivating their work.[28]

The authors look towards Gary Hayes' 2007 blog post and diagram of the myth of Web 2.0 non-participation as a way to debunk the pyramid of participation (see Figure 2.1).[29]

Although Hayes uses the term passive, and does not use the term lurking, he seeks to account for a wider range of participation by disassembling the participation pyramid. He redraws the singular hierarchical structure of the pyramid of participation as two separate triangles. The original pyramid's congruent isosceles triangle becomes two incongruent right triangles whose bases rest one on top of the other. The larger triangle represents the typical activity of participants in the co-creative community and the smaller triangle represents the participation – degree of resonance in the co-creative community. In this model, there are eight possible activities a user can engage in, ranked from low to high content input:

1. passively consuming content;
2. passively consuming content and post *personalizing it*;
3. forwarding and *sharing* content;
4. publicly *rating* content;
5. publicly *commenting* on content;
6. submitting content *created by others*;
7. *editing* content created by others including mashups; and
8. submitting *original* content.

Users engaging in these activities are given the following five identities (also ranked from low to high content input) in the co-creative community:

1. the consumers;
2. the sharers;
3. the critics;
4. the editors; and
5. the creators.

Figure 2.1: The myth of Web 2.0 non-participation

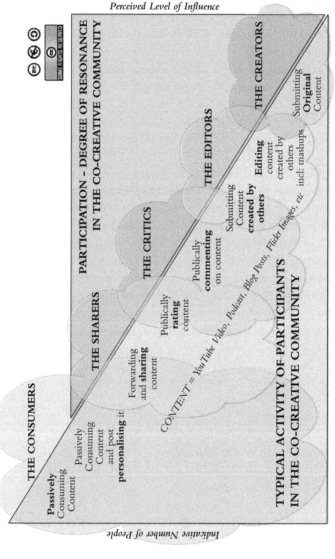

Source: G. Hayes (2007) The myth of Web 2.0 non-participation. Personalize Media. https://www.personalizemedia.com/the-myth-of-non-participation-in-web-20-social-networks/

Importantly, Hayes draws a wavy circle around each identity to indicate the fluid ways in which some activities overlap between more than one identity. This Venn diagram effect underscores that each identity is not fixed; however, it also binds a user's identity to its directly adjacent identities and activities. For example, one could oscillate between sharer and critic, but is unable (in this depiction) to oscillate between sharer and creator. Astutely, he labels the adjacent side of the participation-degree of resonance in the co-creative community right triangle as the 'perceived level of influence'. By choosing the word perceived he allows for the possibility that a sharer and a creator could have the same degree of influence. Notably, the consumers who engage in participation that is only 'consumptive', and do not overlap with the sharers, barely register in the resonance triangle. The consumer identity floats high above both triangles, implying that consumptive behaviour is largely irrelevant.

Scholarly attention is beginning to turn towards broadening the ways that passively consuming content can be measured. Nicole Ellison et al introduce the following diagram in their study of clickers versus lurkers (see Figure 2.2).[30] They define clickers as people who choose to engage in publicity metrics (liking, sharing, commenting) and lurkers as people who do not. The participation of clickers and lurkers is measured in relation to interacting and viewing. Notably, Ellison et al do not distinguish between viewing and reading content. In other words, it is beyond the scope of this particular study to examine the depth to which one has read (for example, scanning versus deeper comprehension) and what meanings were inferred from the process. In this model a person can be highly engaged whether or not they are a lurker or a clicker. The interactivity measured by this model

Figure 2.2: Social media use conceptual categories

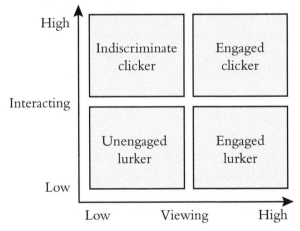

Source: N.B. Ellison et al (2020) Why we don't click: Interrogating the relationship between viewing and clicking in social media contexts by exploring the 'non-click', *Journal of Computer-Mediated Communication*, 25(6), pp. 402–426.

refers to interactivity that occurs on the platform and this particular study does not examine the kinds of interactions that might occur offline.

Where literacy studies can assist is by offering perspective on the socially situated experiences of each individual reader along this continuum of participation. Rosenblatt's work on transactional literacy pre-dates the rise of social networking technologies and the study of digital literacies; however, this does not mean that her work is not relevant. In the transactional theory of reading, Rosenblatt states that 'every reading act is an event, or a transaction involving a particular reader and a particular pattern of signs, and a text, occurring at a particular time in a particular context'.[31] Semioticians like Ferdinand de Saussure explain that meaning-making occurs through a dyadic process of signified and signifier,[32] and Charles Sanders Peirce expands this to a triadic process by emphasizing the additional importance of the sign.[33] For example, when we see the singular word apple that word is a sign that sends a signified message to the brain for how to translate that word into an image and how to develop associations for that image. Each reader will have a uniquely signified image in their brain; a reader might see a red fruit, a green fruit, or a laptop computer. As a reader experiences a full sentence the meaning of the sentence as a whole is a negotiation of signified images, which creates an interpretation. Rosenblatt asserts that within this linguistic processing, 'language is always internalised by a human being transacting with a particular environment'.[34] Therefore 'the text serves as more than a set of stimuli or a pattern of stimuli; it is also a guide or continuing control during the process by which the reader selects, organises and synthesises – in short, interprets – what has emerged from his relationship with the verbal symbols'.[35] The verbal symbols on the page show up within a reader's 'experiential reservoir' of personal, social, historical, and political influences – the computer or the fruit – thus this relationship between text and reader is not fixed, but continually shifting and evolving. Therefore, the reader in literacy studies has an identity that is intersectional, not homogenized.[36]

Meaning is influenced by not just the lived experiences that the reader embodies when encountering a text, it is also the circumstances under which a reader encounters the text that encourage a response along the continuum of efferent or aesthetic experience. In other words, a text can be consumed for:

- efferent purposes, as in reading the label off of a medicine bottle to discern the appropriate dosage; or
- aesthetic purposes, as in immersing in the story of *Jane Eyre*; or
- some combination of efferent and aesthetic purposes.

The reader's stance, efferent or aesthetic, depends upon the way the reader encounters the text and the lived experience of the reader. The interpretation created by the reader's transaction alters the text and the transactional theory of reading provides a lens whereby these textual alterations become visible. Meaning is at once public and private. A public meaning might include a quest to ascertain facts, to unravel literal denotations or interpretations. A private meaning might include a personal connection rooted in one's history, culture, or the point in time when the reading event occurs.

In Figure 2.3, showing Rosenblatt's Efferent–Aesthetic Continuum,[37] she presents four possible positions that one can experience during a reading event. A reading event is the moment one encounters a text. More

Figure 2.3: The Efferent–Aesthetic Continuum: reader's stance in transactions with texts

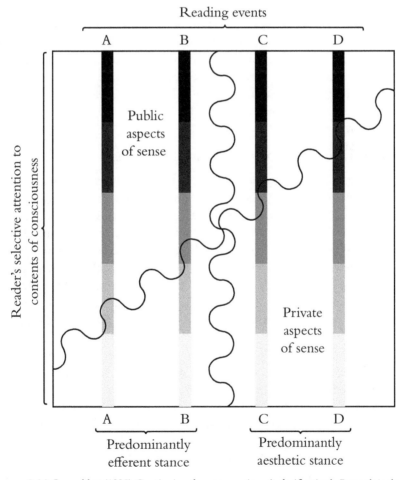

Source: L.M. Rosenblatt (1995) Continuing the conversation: A clarification', *Research in the Teaching of English*, 29(3), pp 349–354. Copyright 1995 by the National Council of Teachers of English. Reprinted with permission.

recent scholarship has begun to describe this moment as a literacy event to encompass texts that include digital media.[38] One can be:

- a reader whose stance is predominately efferent, and whose attention oscillates among public and private aspects of sense, but is mostly public;
- a reader whose stance is predominately efferent, and whose attention oscillates among public and private aspects of sense, but is slightly less public;
- a reader whose stance is predominately aesthetic, and whose attention oscillates among public and private aspects of sense, but is slightly less private; and
- a reader whose stance is predominately aesthetic, and whose attention oscillates among public and private aspects of sense, but is mostly private.

Both Hayes' model and Rosenblatt's model make use of waves. The intersection of the wavy lines indicate the possibility of being between stances and between public and private actions. This is key because our positions are never fixed. They continue to oscillate particularly as the internet-of-things increasingly reifies our everyday objects – watches, refrigerators – into opportunities to engage in participatory culture, thus expanding the number of literacy events we experience each day.

Transactional Theory of New Literacies

The Transactional Theory of New Literacies I am proposing takes Rosenblatt's Efferent–Aesthetic Continuum for print-based texts and turns it towards reading and engaging with networked media. By titling this model the Efferent–Aesthetic Continuum for New Literacies I am specifically signalling to both New Literacies and the New Literacies Studies. If you are reading this as a media scholar or someone whose background is outside the field of literacy studies, the separated nomenclature might seem a bit bonkers. New Literacies can be a way to refer to emerging technologies. But technologies at the vanguard, as Michelle Knobel and Colin Lankshear point out, are sometimes used to reproduce the same effects as earlier tools.[39] For example, one might use a computer to compose rather than a pen because the process is more efficient. However, one's use of the computer might not significantly alter the composition process. In this sense, when I use the term New Literacies, I am referring to emerging technologies that may or may not be used in novel or avant-garde ways. My use of the term New Literacies is also meant to align with the theoretical positions put forth by the New London Group that the New Literacies Studies marks

a shift from literacy to literacies, especially in relation to how people view texts as being situated in different contexts that in turn support different kinds of reading and writing. New, not in the sense of a replacement metaphor, but new in the sense that social, economic, cultural, intellectual, and institutional changes are continually at work.[40]

Media scholars may be familiar with the term 21st-century literacies, which is sometimes conflated or used interchangeably with New Literacies; however, the ILA prefers the use of New Literacies. Referencing the work of 'Don Leu and other experts, the term *new literacies* is preferred because the essential aspect of this new world of literacy is that technologies, and the ways they are used, continually change and generate even newer forms of literacy'.[41] Literacies as a plurality inscribes the act as ever-evolving and never static.

A person who encounters a literacy event on social media might read from a mostly efferent or a mostly aesthetic stance. Both the efferent and aesthetic stances can range from indiscriminate to engaged. This reading process between indiscriminate and engaged is fluid and not fixed. Our attention is constantly shifting. N. Katherine Hayles' article, 'Hyper and deep attention: The generational divide in cognitive modes', introduces the concept of hyperattention, which refers to 'switching focus rapidly among different tasks, preferring multiple information streams, seeking a high level of stimulation, and having a low tolerance for boredom'. This kind of attention yields what scholar James Sosnowski refers to as 'hyperreading', an ability to move quickly and fluidly through a variety of texts because readers are gleaning information from the surface of the text rather than a deeper, closer reading.[42] This hyperreading or surface reading is contrasted with the pedagogical close reading made popular by literary scholar I.A. Richards. For example, one can be engaged in an aesthetic stance while hyperreading or close reading or fluidly moving through both processes. Sosnowski describes a variety of hyperreading practices such as filtering, skimming, pecking, and imposing (among others) that can be utilized in an academic setting.

Where Rosenblatt uses public and private to refer to internal and external meaning-making, in the case of digital literacy, in the case of Figure 2.4 I am applying the terms to the networked audience. As a member of the networked audience one can choose among a range of public and private acts of participation. Public participation registers on the front end of the platform in the form of likes, shares, comments, and content creation. Private participation registers on the back end as hovering, impressioning, and clicking. Private participation can also include literacy practices that take place offline, but are influenced by what has been read online.

Chapters 3 and 4 will discuss the literacy practices people utilize while lurking and the gratifications they seek. I refer to these thematic gratifications as lurker literacies. My use of the word lurker is as an adjective to describe the literacies rather than as a noun to identify a person with the fixed position

Figure 2.4: The Efferent–Aesthetic Continuum of New Literacies

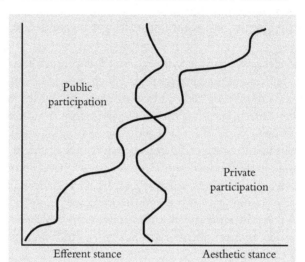

of consistent lurking. Where this book will address five specific lurker literacies – receptive reading, sensemaking, participatory restraint, protective curation, and reflexive entertainment – it bears repeating that this is not an exhaustive list. These lurker literacies mark the start of a conversation about the participatory and valuable ways that lurking impacts platforms, communities, individuals, and society.

3

"To Let Others Know They Are Not Alone": Lurking and Community

In the early 2010s the internet was awash with what have been dubbed Conspiracy Keanu memes[1] featuring a screengrab from the 1989 movie *Bill and Ted's Excellent Adventure*.[2] The absurd story of *Bill and Ted's Excellent Adventure* is set pre-internet; the phone booth, which in a silent nod to *Dr. Who* acts as a time travel portal, is still a piece of cutting-edge technology. It is a film about two California teenage slackers who dream of starting a band called Wyld Stallyns. Their bromance and musical aspirations are threatened when Ted's father insists that if Ted fails his upcoming history exam he will be sent to military school in Alaska. As part of this delusional inciting incident, Bill and Ted are approached by Rufus, an Emissary from the Future, to travel back in time through the phone booth time machine to kidnap key historical figures to assist with the research for their oral history project. Rufus portends that in the future Wyld Stallyns will be a band so significant that their music will end all war, poverty, and promote a 'universal harmony'.

In this screen-shotted scene, Ted, portrayed by Keanu Reeves, has travelled back to the Middle Ages and realizes that he and Bill are about to be attacked by a medieval knight, hence the look of fear and disbelief on Reeves' face. As a meme, Conspiracy Keanu is, much like the premise of *Bill and Ted*, all about the absurd. The variations on this meme, which can be quickly generated on sites like Imgflip, speculate on the construction and purpose of the universe and usually begin with the phrase 'What if?'[3] The most frequently cited one on the meme sites is a slightly paranoid, stoner-style, interrogative 'What if all the specs we see in the light are all miniature universes?' The lurker version of the Conspiracy Keanu meme poses this question, 'What if there are tons of really nice people on the internet and the nicest thing they can do is not comment?' Given the extensive research about the normality of lurking, of people resisting the urge to comment, what if, in this instance, Keanu's question is not so absurd?

What are people doing, thinking, and feeling when they engage in a continuum of private participation from an efferent or aesthetic stance on social media? Could lurking ever be a merciful or necessary silence? In this chapter we will look at a study of neighbourhood Facebook groups and the lurker literacies that arise from the gratifications sought by lurking. Specifically, the chapter will address receptive reading, protective curation, participatory restraint, and reflexive entertainment as lurker literacies that contribute to communities on and offline. It will also offer insights into the literacy practices people use while lurking.

Reading is a sociocultural practice; its effects can be seen through literacy events and the literacy practices they produce.[4] A literacy event is visible; it includes participants, settings, artefacts, and activities.[5] It can be, as literacy studies ethnographer Shirley Brice Heath writes, 'any occasion in which a piece of writing is integral to the nature of the participants' interactions and interpretive processes'.[6] In the case of Facebook, this can mean the content of the posts and the commenting threads that invite Facebook account holders to read and/or publicly interact on the platform. A literacy practice is the way in which that comprehension is applied to real-world situations. Importantly, Mary Barton and David Hamilton explain, literacy practices are 'inferred from observable evidence because they include invisible resources, such as knowledge and feelings; they embody social purposes and values and they are part of a constantly changing context both spatial and temporal'.[7] This invisibility they describe can aptly be applied to lurking, because, as is the case of reading social media, these literacy practices can occur offline in settings tangentially connected to the digital realm. The increasing mobile opportunities to engage with social media underscores the importance of thinking about the effects of spatial and temporal influences on our attention to reading. To best understand literacy practices, whether online or offline, scholars often engage ethnographic or qualitative methods to illuminate the data. Through interviews with participants about the lurker literacy practices they use and the gratifications they seek, participants discussed the valuable community contributions of not commenting.

The neighbourhoods

The New York City suburbs are some of the most segregated communities in the United States.[8] In particular, the New York City suburban public school system has been recognized in a study by Doug Ready of Teachers College, Columbia University as one of the top ten segregated school districts in the United States.[9] The New York City suburban public school system is more segregated than most American school districts in the South, which endured decades of Jim Crow legislation legally mandating the separate schooling of Black and White children and the disproportionate allocation of operational educational funds to favour schools that served White children.[10] These cloistered communities grew from post-Second World War policies that incentivized suburbanization of the areas outside of major US cities. Prior to the Second World War, what has become the New York City suburbs were mostly rural communities and included large estates of wealthy industrial magnates. The GI Bill, in particular, offered honourably discharged servicemen the opportunity to apply for low-interest mortgages that would allow them to purchase homes in newly constructed suburban neighbourhoods. The banks supplying these mortgages, and the companies that sold these houses, often had clauses in their contracts that denied Black people mortgages.[11] These policies continued until the Federal Fair Housing Act of 1968, which sought to prohibit discrimination based on race, colour, religion, sex, national origin, familial status, and disability. The structural barriers to integration in the New York City suburbs continue to persist in subtler ways and the result is an area, as the one examined in this study, that contains approximately 60 population-dense towns whose borders directly touch one another, and of those 60, only three or four could be considered predominantly Black. The predominant Whiteness of the area is part of the historical, cultural, and geographic understanding necessary to examining the literacy practices of people who belong to neighbourhood Facebook groups in this region.

A Facebook group is an optional Facebook feature 'for small group communication and for people to share their common interests and express their opinion[s]. Groups allow people to come together around a common cause, issue or activity to organize, express objectives, discuss issues, post photos and share related content'.[12] Individuals who have Facebook accounts may choose to either create or join groups, but participation in a Facebook group is not a required or necessary part of the Facebook experience. A neighbourhood Facebook group is a community created to share information about a specific geographic community. Members include current residents, former residents, prospective residents, and local business owners.

When initially framing my research questions, I sought to engage three specific communities where I had previously established personal connections and where I would meet the geographic criteria for group membership. I also joined larger regional groups that represented the wider suburban area. I have pseudonymized these three central communities as Ocean Ridge, Whitman Circle, and Hollow Junction. All the participant names mentioned in this chapter have also been pseudonymized. Ocean Ridge is a mostly White affluent community. Whitman Circle is a mostly middle-class White community. Hollow Junction is a mostly Black middle-class community. Class is a peculiar subject when discussing the New York City suburbs because the concentrated wealth in this region is much higher than that of the majority of the United States. For example, Hollow Junction has a population of 24,759 and a median household income of US$80,166. Where the median income in Hollow Junction is significantly below that of the specific suburban county in which it resides – US$116,304 – Hollow Junction is also consistently regarded as one of the most affluent Black communities in the United States. The average household income in the United States is US$69,560; for Black families it is US$46,005.

The study I conducted was two-part. It included a community mapping to gather information from the members of the Facebook groups about the literacy practices used while lurking and then one or two follow-up interviews of 30 minutes to 60 minutes to understand the gratifications sought through lurking while engaging in literacy practices in neighbourhood Facebook groups. There were 203 participants in the study and 18 consented to follow-up interviews.

Literacy practices

What kinds of things do people do when they lurk? Do these things count as participation? Are they valuable? These are the questions I was curious about. In devising an instrument to collect data, I looked to Nonnecke's earlier work on lurking. Nonnecke et al in 2003 tried to answer some of these questions when analysing the results of a survey that identified 79 reasons why someone might lurk.[13] The most popular reasons reported being that they:

1. wanted to be anonymous, and preserve privacy and safety;
2. had work-related constraints, for example, employer did want work email address to be used;
3. had too many or too few messages to deal with, that is, too many messages were burdensome, and it was easy to forget low traffic groups;
4. received poor quality messages, for example, messages were irrelevant to the topic or had little information value;
5. were shy about public posting; and
6. had limited time, that is, other things were more important.

In 2004, however, they distilled these reasons into this singular survey question (among several other open-ended questions): If you never post to this online group/community, what are your reasons?[14] The purpose was to determine, with greater specificity, why someone chooses to lurk.

Of the 19 reasons offered to participants, 'Just reading/browsing is enough' was the top response. This survey work, coupled with Nonnecke et al's findings that lurkers provide value because lurkers (a) work at knowing the group, (b) try not to add to the chaos, (c) extend the group, (d) side post, and (e) make a commitment, led me to consider how the descriptions of these values related to literacy studies. Lurkers reported that they engaged in conversations, gathered information, and posted what they learned in other venues. It is from the collected works of Nonnecke that I devised a list of literacy practices that one might utilize when lurking on social media.

I shared this list of literacy practices with participants in the neighbourhood Facebook groups via digital community mapping. Community mapping (sometimes referred to as asset mapping) is both a process and a product where a community collectively and informally self-identifies data to map assets, values, and/or beliefs.[15] When utilized offline, community mapping or asset mapping usually involves inviting community members together to a forum where they list ideas on Post-it notes and to align them under a SWOT (strengths, weaknesses, opportunities, threats) analysis. Members then vote on the notes that they agreed with. For this study, I digitized the community mapping process by utilizing virtual sticky notes via Padlet, a social curation application. Chapter 6 will offer a deeper dive into the intricacies of community mapping and how this method can be useful for gathering data that includes a wider range of participants.

Instead of using SWOT analysis, I instead listed the literacy practices I had devised based on Nonnecke. The digital community mapping process would allow all of the 102,793 members of the 15 local neighbourhood Facebook groups the option to favourite the practices they engaged in and/or add additional practices. Each literacy practice Post-it listed the disclaimer that one should only favourite the practice if they did so without engaging in publicity metrics. For example, 'Listened to a podcast about something I read about in a Facebook group, but did not like, comment, or share content about it'. Although none of the 203 group members who elected to participate in the study added any additional practices, I became aware of additional practices through my discussions with the participants who consented to be interviewed. I added these additional literacy practices to the community mapping. The results can be found in Table 3.1.

The two most popular uses of literacy practices while lurking, search engine research and read for entertainment, indicate that individuals who lurk are making conscious choices about when to engage in publicity metrics that can be seen by other members of the online community and the Facebook platform. Although each practice can fall anywhere along the efferent and aesthetic continuum depending on the individual's experience, I would like to offer some examples of how these literacy practices can exist along the continuum. Search engine research; screenshot posts; understand different point of view; read for investment opportunities; and read for hyperlocal news are efferent information-seeking practices. When choosing to lurk, a person in an efferent stance can be conducting research, curating or

Table 3.1: Use of literacy practices while lurking

Initial practices	Favourites
Search engine research	173
Face-to-face conversation	159
Screenshot posts	159
Text message conversation	157
Support local business	142
Take social action	123
Attend event	86
Watch television show	82
Watch movie	77
Buy book	54
Borrow library book	44
Listen to song	36
Listen to podcast	30
Post to other social networking site	24
Additional practices	**Favourites**
Read for entertainment	172
Understand different point of view	61
Read for investment opportunities	32
Read for hyperlocal news	14

annotating information through the collection of screenshots, and grappling with the comprehension of new ideas. Face-to-face conversation and text message conversation can be from the efferent stance of collecting additional information about a post encountered in the group, but it can quickly slide into the aesthetic stance of gossiping or joking about the posts encountered in the group. A post one has read can inspire them to buy a book or borrow one from a library, listen to a podcast or a song, watch a television show or a movie – all experiences that float along the efferent and aesthetic continuum as one processes information and is perhaps captivated by the aura of the text. Through my interviews with participants, I was able to dig deeper into the gratifications they sought while engaging in these literacy practices and to contextualize them within the geographic location in which they were situated.

Receptive reading

During the time the interviews were conducted in the summer and fall of 2020, there were three major current events that dominated the news cycle and personal discourse: the COVID-19 pandemic, Black Lives Matter and the marches in response to the murder of George Floyd, and the upcoming 2020 US presidential election. As participants discussed their reasons for lurking, they talked about their desire to better understand divergent points of view and a need to verify information. None of the participants from Hollow Junction, the predominantly Black neighbourhood, agreed to be interviewed. Therefore, the participant data from interviews comes from the predominantly White middle- and upper-class neighbourhoods and reflects that perspective. These participants engaged in receptive reading, in part, because discussions of algorithmic bias were becoming more mainstream. Although the Netflix docu-drama movie, *The Social Dilemma*, leaves much to be desired in terms of its scope – narrow focus on White tech industry professionals, and absence of the critical work done by Safiya Noble, Ruha Benjamin, and others – its position as an accessible and easy-to-stream film brought these ideas into the homes of many participants. Participants discussed their realization that their newsfeeds were probably showing them only the opinions of people with similar political, racial, and socioeconomic backgrounds.

Shannon, of Ocean Ridge, described the film's influence by saying, "Facebook is made so you see many opinions that are the same as yours and you start kind of taking that as the majority. ... I started to try and read other people's opinions, so I could be flexible in my thinking." Kristen of Ocean Ridge, a Democrat, expressed a similar sentiment about reading the posts of a Republican neighbour who also attended the same high school as Kristen. She said:

'He's allowed to be Republican. It's not like we can all be so black and white about all this. I like seeing his responses to stuff in particular because I like the way he disagrees. ... He just respectfully disagrees ... and is able to hold a rational discussion. And these days, especially with the friends that I know, not really close friends, but people that I went to high school with, they're just all watching the same channel and they have the same buzzwords. ... It's really just hard to have a conversation with them. So in terms of learning new things, I guess I value his opinions and where they're coming from.'

Logan of Whitman Circle makes the important distinction that the degree of opposition is often an important factor when deciding whether or not to engage in receptive reading. He explains:

'There are plenty of times you read through what people are saying with diametrically opposed political views to your own to at least understand where other folks in the spectrum are coming from. And even more importantly, sometimes you read stuff from people that are not diametrically opposed to you, but have at least enough of a markedly different point of view, that it's valuable to see people from a broad spectrum, not just the two polar opposites.'

To apply what Logan has said to Kristen's point: both Kristen and her conservative high school friend were not Trump supporters. They belonged to two different political parties, but shared their disinterest in re-electing Trump. Therefore, part of what interested her in receptive reading is that she shared some common ground, and wanted to better understand the aspects of conservative political opinion where they differed.

In regard to Black Lives Matter, Claudia of Ocean Ridge, who identifies as a White liberal, explains a similar desire to better understand the movement. She says:

'I don't know if necessarily my opinion has shifted as much as I've been educated by things that I didn't know. Like, whether it be someone sharing their particular experiences … or sharing maybe an article or a data point that I wasn't aware of that has maybe shifted my opinion. … For example, maybe systemic racism wasn't something I was so aware of and now seeing people's comments on these data points. … It makes you feel more strongly.'

Mallory from Whitman Circle expressed a similar sentiment. She did not specify her registered political position, but she is a member of a multigenerational family of law enforcement officers and a gun owner who firmly supports US Second Amendment Rights, which allows private citizens the 'right to bear arms'.[16] She states that she has learned a lot about systemic racism and it is something she was not as informed about. In general, she feels that political discussions should occur face-to-face to avoid "keyboard warriors" people who post inflammatory things they would not say publicly. While she scrolls past derogatory comments from both sides, she was open to learning about systemic racism from posts that were written in a way to "empathise or sympathise with somebody else's perspective".

Sam of Whitman Circle simultaneously engages in lateral reading and receptive reading to verify information. Lateral readers briefly scan an article for information and then browse around to other sites to verify information.[17] Sam doesn't identify as Republican or Democrat, but he reads posts from users on both sides and tries to read news from CNN and Fox to get a broader sense of a story. When he encounters a headline that disturbs him, he researches it on both media outlets to understand the full context. When a friend texted him a screenshot of a post about 'disgusting animals poisoning NYC police officers', he logged on to the neighbourhood Facebook group.

The post described Black Lives Matter supporters putting Clorox bleach in the milkshakes of New York City police officers at a Shake Shack restaurant. When Sam researched the story, he learned that this incident was deemed an accident with the cleaning products in the milkshake machine and it was not a premeditated action, nor was anyone affiliated with Black Lives Matter involved.

Receptive reading about COVID-19 made Anne of Whitman Circle more aware of her socioeconomic privilege. During this time, New York state transitioned from lockdown, and restaurants were reopening for the first time in months. Restaurants were required to adhere to strict guidelines in order to continue operations. This included diners being masked until their food was served and maintaining social distance from other diners not in their party. When New York state indoor dining reopened Anne went to a restaurant and, when served, took off her mask to eat. She saw a friend, and got up from her table to talk. The waitress stopped Anne because she wasn't wearing a mask and explained that she had to stay with her own table. Anne was compliant, but verbally expressed her dissatisfaction with what she felt was a ridiculous policy.

The next day she read a post on the Whitman Circle Facebook group by a restaurant worker begging patrons to understand how difficult it is to work in the restaurant industry under COVID-19 guidelines. The post urged customers not to take their anger out on low-wage employees who work under strict COVID-19 protocols with little job security. Anne did not engage with publicity metrics on the post, but felt that it was speaking to her about the way she had behaved in the restaurant. She talked about the post with her friends and her children, pledging to be more empathetic, and to tip better the next time she went to a restaurant. As we will further explore in Chapter 4, receptive reading is an important first step towards activism, but reading alone is not enough to enact social change.

Participatory restraint

Participants were aware of the power they wield by withholding likes, comments, and shares. This act of participatory restraint was strategically undertaken by some participants to gratify the desire to suppress the spread of information and/or to pivot to offline action.[18] In my discussions with participants some individuals undertook this effort on their own, while others collaborated with group members off-platform via text or phone call to coordinate efforts to suppress information. Resisting Facebook's publicity metrics was a small, but actionable, dissent that one could take in the face of this monolith.

Upper-class neighbourhoods like Ocean Ridge measure their worth, in part, on the ranking and perceived quality of their public school system.

A *good* public school district directly influences property values. And with these increased property values comes higher property and school taxes. The school district budget, which must be voted on and approved by the community taxpayers, was always a contentious topic within the neighbourhood groups in this study. It was in a post where community members were arguing over the size of the school budget that Claudia describes a coordinated act of suppression.

A handful of community members were angered by a parent-led fundraising effort for COVID-19 mitigation supplies. In their opinion these supplies should have been funded by the highly priced school taxes, not from a charity fundraiser. Some group members began to fight with the original poster and commenters to demonstrate the necessity of the supplies. The purpose of these arguments was to persuade readers to see the value in contributing to the fundraiser. As the number of people involved in the discussion grows, so do the number of people reading it. While Claudia is often happy to share her opinion and try to reason with others, she decided to lurk and not engage in publicity metrics. By not engaging with the post, her resistance was part of an effort to minimize algorithmic attention. Virtual learning was an overwhelming experience for Claudia. Keeping the schools safely open was her top priority. For this reason, she felt that the stakes were too high on this particular post. She did not want to offer free advertising to those with views similar to that of the original poster who were not yet aware of the fundraising project. She notes that in offline conversation with other friends, they, too, had chosen to refrain from publicity metrics for the same reason. The post did not receive the traction the original poster intended. The fundraiser successfully met its target goal.

Participatory restraint can also be a way that people prioritize their offline community relationships. Shannon often thinks about how others might interpret her words and images before she posts. Even something seemingly happy or celebratory gives her pause. She often thinks about how the post might affect one's well-being and mental health. Although I'm using the term publicity metrics in this book, to describe overt front-end interactions such as likes, comments, and shares, popular media sometimes refers to them as vanity metrics. Vanity metrics, media scholar Richard Rogers explains, are 'the measurement and display of how well one is doing in the "success theatre" of social media'.[19] The phrase 'success theatre' was coined by Jenna Worthman in a *New York Times* blog post in which she describes the homogenizing focus of social media interactions where users feel they must only share the most 'flattering angle of our faces, our homes, our evenings out, our loved ones and our trips'.[20] She explains that users are cautious of how what they post can have an impact on future relationships and career prospects.

For Shannon, she knows that she sometimes gets jealous or anxious when scrolling through her newsfeed. She described a post where a friend had recently been to the beach and shared a photo of the umbrella and ocean view. It seemed idyllic and Shannon had been quarantining at home. She decided to reach out to her friend offline to learn more about the beach visit. At the time of the interview not much was known about how COVID-19 spread. Was it airborne? Was it ever safe to be outside without a mask? Shannon questioned whether or not she was being too restrictive with her family. When talking to her friend on the phone she learned that the visit had been brief. It takes an hour, round trip, to reach the ocean. The friend stayed at the beach only an hour, not long enough to eat or need to use the restroom. They did not swim, but rather walked along the beach and admired the ocean from the chairs underneath their umbrella. They wore masks and tried to remain six feet or more away from the few other people at the beach. Shannon felt better, less anxious, knowing the full context for the picture. But she worries about other people who do not make the gesture to contextualize posts that make them feel unsettled. She is concerned by the ways her teenagers and even some of her friends get depressed comparing themselves to others.[21] The small business she owns requires a social media presence, but other than posting to promote her work, she doesn't want to add to someone else's sorrow and refrains from posting anything personal. She engages in participatory restraint to diminish the disproportionate attention that vanity metrics play on our psyche. For her, it is a way of letting others know that they are not alone.

Other times participants wished to extend the online conversation with friends in more meaningful ways. Elizabeth of Ocean Ridge is a proud Trump supporter and, at the time of the interview, hopes that he will be re-elected in 2020. However, not all of her offline friends share her opinion. She encountered a post in an Ocean Ridge Facebook group that listed all of the things that Trump achieved during his tenure. Despite her commitment to his campaign, she was sceptical that all of the things listed were true. She decided to not immediately use publicity metrics for two reasons: first, if some of the information turned out to be false, spreading the information could sour Trump's reputation for undecided voters; second, even if the information is true, registered Democrats and Independents are not likely to change their opinion by reading the post. This would be the kind of post where people would argue and become further entrenched in their beliefs. She purposefully did not engage in publicity metrics to suppress the spread of the post.

Where Elizabeth did not dissent the original post, she did dissent to the commenting thread where there was vociferous bickering and did not want to expand the reach of the debate. Elizabeth decided to fact-check all of the items on the post and was pleased that they appeared to be true.

She printed three copies of the post and called two friends, one who was a Democrat and one who was an Independent, to invite them over for a socially distanced meetup in her backyard. During their visit, Elizabeth passed out a copy of the post for each friend to read. Elizabeth and her friends engaged in a discussion of Trump's accomplishments. The friends did not agree that all items were necessarily celebratory accomplishments, but they did concede that some things like increased funding for the arts was important.[22] Elizabeth is not certain how both of her friends will vote in the 2020 presidential election, but having this kind of discussion offline, face-to-face, was a way to sustain their friendship and local community ties. It also limited the spread of the misinformation that occurred among those bickering in the commenting section.

Participants were well aware of the White homogeneity of their community and the implicitly (and sometimes explicitly) racist views that can be expressed by their neighbours. Kristen and Shannon of Ocean Ridge state that the neighbourhood group is where they first learned about a series of attempted assaults of a possibly sexual nature. Initially the incidents were discussed in the Facebook group and it took several days for the local media to publish the story. In the interim, Facebook group members shared information on the specific streets and times of day when the attempts occurred. The assailant's clothes were described, but no other identifying details. One of the clothing items the assailant allegedly wore was a hooded sweatshirt. Shannon was hesitant to comment on these posts even though she wanted more information. Pressing for more information might reveal the race of the assailant and even though she was nervous, she did not want to inadvertently contribute to a post that might amplify a response of racial profiling among community members. The hooded sweatshirt, or hoodie, has been a symbol of the unjust profiling of young Black men since the murder of 17-year-old Trayvon Martin in 2012.[23]

Protective curation

Participants described reading and curating information as a way to gratify a desire to protect their socioeconomic status. This includes gathering information to professionally advance in one's career, and to maintain the perceived quality of community life. In regard to professional advancement, participants sought neighbourhood information that would be valuable to the growth and development of their businesses. Kristen, of Ocean Ridge, will sometimes find herself scrolling through her Facebook feed and encountering a post that might be useful to her husband who sells steel. When she reads a post about newly proposed construction, she will show him her phone and they will have a face-to-face discussion about whether or not he should make a bid to provide the materials.

Abby, of Whitman Circle, is a realtor and finds that her neighbourhood groups are a great place to 'listen in' and uses it as 'market research' on what prices people are willing to pay for homes, and what kind of features they desire in a home. She cites the LIEB CAST podcast, which recently amplified this idea in a podcast titled 'Real estate opportunities by location in 2020 and 2021'.[24] Although she has been using neighbourhood Facebook groups for market research for years, she thought that it was interesting that the pandemic had encouraged not just realtors themselves, but higher-level investors to begin joining groups like Upper West Side Moms, a Facebook group for mothers who live on the wealthy Upper West Side of Manhattan, to curate information.[25] Lieb and Lieb encouraged investors to think about how the pandemic will influence the patterns of migration for wealthy New York City homeowners. They encouraged their podcast listeners to join groups like Upper West Side Moms or Upper East Side Moms and 'listen in' to which ex-urban geographic areas were becoming more desirable and to think about how they could (a) scale their businesses to meet the needs of these wealthy migrants, (b) offer venture capital to companies uniquely positioned to serve these demographics, or (c) buy stock in goods and services that target the ex-urban community.[26] The efficacy of this curation strategy is confirmed by other participants who explained that they sought the Ocean Ridge and Whitman Circle neighbourhood Facebook groups as a way to vet the community before purchasing their home. They sought information on the local school district, the personal values of their potential neighbours, and the range of services and businesses offered by the community.

By lurking, participants also sought to protect their current professional position in the hopes of professional future advancement. Participants who were small business owners felt reluctant to engage in publicity metrics because they feared professional reprimand. Professional reprimand is when a comment, like, or share leads to a negative professional consequence from an employer or prospective client. As Anne of Ocean Ridge explains, "I would prefer that people felt that they could come to me if they needed my services. And not [think], 'well, I don't want to go to a liberal progressive'." Sam, of Whitman Circle, who works for his family-owned business, says, "I've always had the mindset: if you have nothing to hide, then, who cares? ... But nowadays you gotta watch what you post. They could screenshot what you wrote." He explains that a screenshot can be enough to harm the reputation of his business. Mallory, of Whitman Circle, is aware that the superintendent of the school where she works makes note of things as seemingly trivial as a faculty member liking a status celebrating a snow day, a day when severe weather conditions force a school to temporarily close. Colleagues' posts have been screen-shotted by other community members and then submitted to the school district with the submitter urging the superintendent to reprimand the teacher. While Mallory is certain that political posts are potentially damaging, the snow day posts made her realize that any interaction could be twisted to be deemed inappropriate. She said:

'I don't see a problem with saying, "Yay: It's a snow day!" Everybody likes snow days … but evidently in [the superintendent's] mind this makes people look like they don't love their job, which makes you unprofessional. How people interpret your words becomes your problem. And I don't need any more problems.'

Participants collected information that would improve their quality of life in their local community. For example, participants often refer to their neighbourhood Facebook groups to contextualize the noise of sirens or helicopters and to obtain safety information. Abby, of Whitman Circle, will read through her Facebook feed first thing in the morning and pay attention to posts about accidents or traffic queries to determine the safest and fastest route to work. After a series of attempted sexual assaults in the Ocean Ridge neighbourhood, participants relied on neighbourhood groups to track which streets, at what time of day, the attempted assaults occurred. This information was then used to determine when and where to jog, walk dogs, or engage in other outdoor pursuits.

Participants supported local businesses as a way to preserve the local economy, which in turn maintains property values in the community. During the New York state imposed lockdown, participants relied on their neighbourhood Facebook groups to determine what restaurants were still open for takeout and delivery in their community. The desire to support these restaurants was twofold. Participants wanted to reduce the risk of COVID-19 by ordering food for contactless pickup, but they also wanted to ensure that local businesses survived the pandemic lockdown. Abby of Whitman Circle would take note of open restaurants with Family Meal Deals: large portions of food that could be eaten over the course of several meals, and call them to order dinner. She discovered restaurants she had never tried before and told her neighbours and friends about them via socially distant conversation or text messages, encouraging them to try them out. Anne, from Ocean Ridge, saw a post from another neighbourhood group, beyond the scope of this study, that advertised a 'bar crawl' supporting three local restaurants. Participants could order a 'bar crawl' and would receive a delivery order of three appetisers and three alcoholic drinks from three different local restaurants. After reading about this, she thought it was a clever idea and she called a restaurant in Ocean Ridge to tell them about it and to suggest that they plan a similar event to raise community spirits and support the restaurant industry. She never engaged in publicity metrics on any of the Facebook pages associated with these restaurants. Most notably, she is not professionally affiliated with any restaurants and would not directly profit from this event.

Participants sought information not covered in great depth by their local newspaper. Jessica, of Ocean Ridge, feels Facebook has become her 'neighbourhood newspaper'. She appreciates the opportunity to hear directly from primary sources, naming the group's coverage of the community's privatized water utility supplier as an exemplar. After it was revealed that the privatized water had a high level of contaminants, there was a grassroots campaign to develop an Ocean Ridge public water utility. By lurking on these discussions, Jessica was able to make choices for her family about whether or not to upgrade their water filtration system and to identify the local political candidates who support these issues.

Reflexive entertainment

When discussing the gratifications sought by social media interaction, entertainment is often revealed to be one of the top reasons.[27] Lurking, while seeking entertainment, oscillates along the efferent and aesthetic continuum in ways that are different from those engaging in receptive reading, protective curation, or participatory restraint. For example, one might lean more efferent in stance as they engage in protective curation, seeking to collect information about the pollutants in the local water supply. This act of protective curation might also trigger an offline aesthetic response where one will discuss their personal fears and concerns with a friend via face-to-face, phone, or text message conversation. In my conversations with participants, however, those engaging in protective curation did not question or interrogate their motives. This was also true for those engaging in receptive reading and participatory restraint. Whereas those participants who sought entertainment through lurking were aware of the dangers of being a bystander and questioned the limits of their laughter. By naming this theme reflexive entertainment, I am drawing on the theory of reflexive thinking. Sociologist Anthony Giddens posits that our social activities are 'a reflexive project of the self' whereby our bodies are constantly revising our identities in response to changing social dynamics.[28] This is not to be confused with educational theorist John Dewey's ideas on reflection as active, persistent, and intentional.[29] Reflexive entertainment is not intentional in so much as it is a continuum from ambience to engagement. It is through the theatrics of popcorn munching while the comments unfold that participants began to question themselves as social actors.

Claudia, who regularly engages in publicity metrics in her Ocean Ridge neighbourhood Facebook groups, also belongs to a large regional parents' group and chooses to lurk in that group because the content can sometimes be "raunchy". The membership numbers of the group clock in at several thousand. She said, "[I am] shocked by how many people I know are in it and comment. I read their stuff and [I think to myself] I never saw that about you." The possibility of encountering the name of a neighbour writing about a lascivious topic they might not otherwise discuss in a face-to-face environment is amusing. It is the type of entertainment Claudia might seek out if she is waiting in the car to pick up her children from school or for a few seconds of downtime while her kids are engaged in play. Since the membership numbers in this group are so high, she is not too concerned about her laughter. It is other groups where the membership numbers are smaller and more localized that she is conscious of the role she may play as a bystander. When comments in a different local group turned antisemitic, she felt it was important to engage in publicity metrics to dissent the vicious laughter.

Mallory and Sam joined the Whitman Circle Facebook group primarily to laugh, particularly when they are at work. Mallory described Whitman Circle as full of "pistol people", which she defined as people who are quick to start a fight. She compared this kind of entertainment to watching a Larry David comedic sitcom that is humorous, yet simultaneously uncomfortable. She said, "It's hilarious, but you're almost like anxious because you know someone is going to be such an asshole to someone, you know? And it's funny, but it's anxiety inducing. It's really not good. It's addictive, but not good for you." Sam, in Whitman Circle, described a similar sentiment, "You see people arguing, and they're trying to be very calm and relaxed and everything. And then you see someone else just like hammering away at them and I just want to be like, 'that's just so unnecessary'." These exchanges are often among neighbours he does not know personally. When asked if he does intervene, Sam replied in the negative. Sam does identify some of these exchanges to be "bullying", but since it is bullying between two consenting adults, he does not feel a sense of guilt in reading these exchanges for pleasure. Since Mallory's work had turned remote due to COVID-19, and she found herself spending an increased amount of time reading the comments as an interactive "soap opera". Once remote work ended, she found herself less willing to just sit back and read and eager to seek entertainment from novels and fictionalized settings. She was beginning to question whether or not it was healthy to spend so much time engrossed in other people's drama.

Logan described lurking for entertainment in Whitman Circle as "mindless entertainment" that requires less time commitment than starting a television show or a movie. For him, it is the full-text, printed, nature of comments that makes it appealing. This is the kind of entertainment he engages in while commuting by railroad and his commute is the only time he has available for leisurely reading or viewing digital content. There can be buffering delays while in transit that make it difficult to watch a movie or television show. To be polite in the shared commuting space, the volume of the television show or movie must be turned down, even with headphones on. The ability to put your eyes to the screen and start consuming rather than having to wait for the video download also may make this kind of entertainment appealing. Logan likened the process of just reading the comments to "having a look at a traffic accident, while you're driving." He said it is a "guilty indulgence."

Although he mostly lurks in the Whitman Circle group, he found himself compelled to comment on a meme titled 'Vote Joe and the Ho'.[30] The meme was posted after (then) Democratic presidential nominee Joseph Biden chose Kamala Harris as his running mate.

The meme pictures Biden and Harris shoulder to shoulder in a picture taken from a car. The text has two lines. The top line in smaller print reads: 'Vote Joe and the Ho'. The bottom line in larger font reads: '2020'. Community members laughed at the meme and made snide comments. Logan said he was deeply affected by the death of Supreme Court Justice Ruth Bader Ginsberg and, when he encountered this meme, he felt compelled to respond. He commented on the thread that the comments were racist and misogynistic. As he told me:

'On one level it's just unbelievably offensive, but honestly, I suspect that there is probably a little bit of a feedback loop going here. I have a suspicion that talking to you previously made me give a little bit more [pause] I was not willing to just drive by without commenting. ... There's a lot of nonsense and conspiracy theory and whatnot [on this Facebook page]. And [sometimes] you just have to shake your head and walk on by because you can't engage with everything. And then you have to find some line where you figure, this is, you know, the line where if I don't say something, then how complicit am I in this?'

Although he chose to delurk on this particular post, he did so, aware that others who were lurking would read what he wrote. He didn't want the commenting thread to only be filled with hateful words.

Limitations

The literacy practices identified in this study are by no means an exhaustive list. Further studies should seek to demonstrate how frequently these self-reported literacy practices occur and in what contexts. This might require the use of eye-tracking camera technologies to observe participants as they are reading. Or it might require participants to include specific examples of posts they read that inspired the action taken (for example, a post that inspired a charitable donation or led to the purchase of a book). Further studies should seek to examine lurker literacies on other kinds of Facebook groups and social media platforms. A major limitation of this study is the lack of diversity of interview participants. New York City suburbs are some of the most segregated areas in the United States (Winslow, 2019). It is essential to replicate the interview portion of this study in communities where Whiteness is not dominant.

The introduction of receptive reading, participatory restraint, protective curation, and reflexive entertainment add to the collective research on the valuable and participatory ways that lurkers contribute to online and offline communities. Through lurking, participants sought to gratify desires to:

1. understand a divergent point of view;
2. verify information;
3. suppress the spread of information;
4. pivot to offline social action;
5. advance professionally; and
6. maintain quality of community life.

These themes, and the narrative data included in the study that supports them, underscore the complexity of the decision of when to lurk.

Moderators play an important role in creating communities and encouraging or even in some cases mandating the adoption of lurker literacies. Chapter 4 will explore these themes.

Copyright notice

"Aint That Special": Moderating in the Age of Digital Exploitation

As one of the most popular meme templates, there are a seemingly infinite number of snarky Gene Wilder faces floating around the internet on any given day. The 'Aint that special' meme is often used as a way to express scepticism at one's supercilious attitude or antics.[1] The Facebook moderator version includes the top title 'Your [*sic*] a Facebook moderator' and the bottom title 'Aint [*sic*] that special' overlaid on a screenshot of the condescending face of Wilder's portrayal of Willy Wonka from the 1971 movie *Willy Wonka and the Chocolate Factory*.[2] Although Wilder's depiction of Willy Wonka highlights his lofty, and at times patronizing, attitude towards the Golden Ticket-winning children and their families, this screengrab is from a moment of genuine sincerity and enthusiasm.

In the moments prior to this screenshot, Willy Wonka is about to introduce the Everlasting Gobstopper, an important symbol in both the movie and the Roald Dahl book from which the movie originates. The Everlasting Gobstopper is a candy 'for children with very little pocket money. You can suck 'em forever … and they never get any smaller. Never'.[3] This candy serves a dual social purpose: it gives children with lower socioeconomic status access to a luxury item and it is a test for the Golden Ticket-winning children to discern who among them is trustworthy. Willy Wonka has devised a verbal contract with each child to take one Gobstopper, keep it for themselves, and 'never show [the Everlasting Gobstopper] to another living soul' as long as they shall live. It's a contrived situation. Each child believes they have been offered a bribe by Arthur Slugworth, a rival candymaker, to steal an Everlasting Gobstopper. However, Wonka has asked Mr Wilkinson, an employee of the Willy Wonka Chocolate Factory, to pose as Slugworth and offer each child a bribe. Charlie, the poorest of the Golden Ticket children, ultimately resists the bribe and returns his Everlasting Gobstopper to Willy Wonka, winning the keys to the factory. The Everlasting Gobstopper is a symbol of virtue and the screenshot expression of Wilder's face is earnest.

When thinking about this meme in relation to Facebook moderators, the juxtaposition of what at first glance appears to be Wilder's wide-eyed scepticism with the 'Aint that special' title is what makes us laugh. We chuckle because moderators are the de facto rulers of the Facebook group who wield the power to control the flow of conversation in the group, set the rules, and restrict the membership. These powers, however, are castrated by the unpaid and voluntary nature of the position. Hence the cynicism of using 'Aint', a word that already has a complex grammatical history of demarcating social class and access to capital, both social and economic. Adding insult to injury, the meme title contains several common usage errors (the omission of the apostrophe in 'Aint' and 'your' instead of you're). But moderators, like the Everlasting Gobstopper from which this scene is clipped, are incredibly special. In my discussions with participants about their decisions to lurk, the moderator, and how they govern their group, influences the degree to which a person will visibly participate in a group. The moderator also creates the conditions upon which participants feel that they are part of a community. However, the working conditions of moderators have an effect on their ability to govern their groups. Moderating might begin as an act of passion, but it can often lead to burnout. Despite being an unpaid position, the work moderators perform can require round-the-clock, seven-days-a-week attention. In terms of Facebook groups, there is no formal required professional development programme that trains one to be a moderator. The experience can be isolating and overwhelming. These working conditions shape the tone and tenor of the group.

In this chapter we'll look at three types of Facebook groups: affinity groups, health groups, and neighbourhood groups. Scholars who study lurking have routinely cited learning communities and health-based communities as places where lurking is beneficial.[4] Neighbourhood groups where members are often connected both on and offline are also important spaces to better understand how online governance has reverberations in the offline world. The names of the moderators and participants interviewed have been pseudonymized as per the institutional review board (IRB) approved consent form signed by participants before the interview was conducted. This chapter will explore two key questions: What makes a good moderator? And what do moderators need to be successful in their roles? And through exploring these questions, we'll look at three lurker literacies influenced by moderation: receptive reading, sensemaking, and participatory restraint.

Affinity groups

When the result of the 2016 US presidential election was determined and Donald Trump was declared the winner, supporters of opponent Hilary

Clinton's Democratic campaign were devastated. Clinton's supporters took to the secret Facebook group Pantsuit Nation to express their grief, outrage, and to seek solidarity with other link-minded supporters. Pantsuit Nation, founded in late October 2016, as an invite-only secret affinity group for supporters of Clinton's presidential campaign, had over 2.5 million members.[5] On election day, many members donned pantsuits as a nod to Clinton's signature style, often mocked by her opponents as unfeminine and a symbol of a nasty woman.[6] Inside the secret group, some of the members shared their experiences as Black women in America and the commenting threads became a space dominated by the replies of White women.

According to Mary, a White member of the Pantsuit Nation Facebook group, the responding White women were dominating the posts and replying before carefully considering the ways in which their privilege shaped their opinions and experiences. Mary had deep expertise in the area of moderation and felt compelled to interject and assist. In her professional life, Mary has been an anti-racism trainer alongside working in the education and the divinity sectors. In her retelling, Mary replied, "Please step back on this post and let people of colour speak. … You get all the other posts to talk. It's just one. You live with it and move on," and in her description of the response she received, she said the "outcry of outrage by White people was crazy." Jane, a Black member of Pantsuit Nation, was frustrated by what had within the space of a few weeks become an unsafe space for members who are women of colour to speak to their own experiences of feminism. She decided to leave the group and form her own secret group that centred the experiences of women of colour and their allies. Jane took note of Mary's role in attempting to moderate the voices of White women and the absence of such moderation from the official group moderators. Jane invited Mary to join her in her new endeavour and Mary agreed. To protect the privacy of the group and its members, the group will hereafter be referred to as the Alliance Group.

The Alliance Group, which began as an offshoot of Pantsuit Nation, quickly became its own independent entity. It was conceived as a space for women to work together by centring the experiences of women of colour, while also allowing space for some White allies to participate. The Alliance Group was intentionally designed to be a space where members could work together. Initially many White women wanted to join this group and the group's membership numbers began to swell. According to Mary, when White women were accepted into the group they would "jump on a thread saying things that were really painful to women of colour" and when they were called out about their actions by the moderator they would "float away", sometimes with a dramatic speech before removing themselves from the group.

Required receptive reading

In this group, receptive reading is required practice to help White participants negotiate their 'willful ignorance' of the lived experiences of people of colour and to develop allyship before becoming active contributors to the discussion posts.[7] Jane realized that the Alliance Group needed a way to train its White members on how to participate and engage as an ally in online spaces. This would mean that participants should remain 'strategically silent' before inserting themselves into the conversation.[8] First, Jane decided that the group needed to expand its moderators and she invited Mary to become a moderator to specifically work with White group members. Next, Jane developed an intricate network of Facebook groups, which she refers to as rooms. This is not to be confused with the rooms Facebook feature which allows for video chat and conferencing. Rather she took the metaphor of a house and created one Facebook group and designated each room within the house for specific members to talk and learn together. The rooms of the Alliance Group aim to make space for everyone (Figure 4.1). Some rooms are exclusively for women of colour, some rooms are specifically for White women, and other rooms are open to allies of any race.

Jane was drawn to the metaphor of a house as a way to make visible the act of construction that is necessary to build a better world. To build something, you have to be willing to do the construction work.

The entryway or door to the community is a public Facebook group that is accessible to anyone with a Facebook account. When someone decides they would like to enter the rest of the house, there are two paths. Women of colour (this includes people who are trans or nonbinary and who identify as a woman) are admitted immediately upon request. The living room is a

Figure 4.1: Rooms in the Alliance Group network of Facebook groups

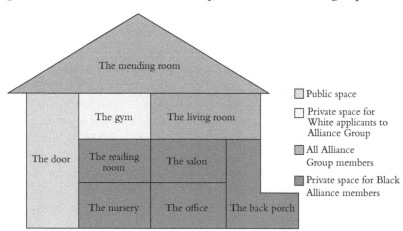

space for all members to talk together. There are several Black only spaces: the kitchen, to share recipes; the office, to discuss Black owned small businesses; the nursery, to discuss parenting; the reading room, for book clubs; the salon, to learn about the history of structural racism; the back porch, a place for free talk on any topic. When devising the rooms, Jane was concerned about White members choosing to lurk in the women of colour only spaces. She devised separate groups in order to create places for women of colour members to be psychologically safe and vulnerable. To centre Black women's experience means that you honour and respect their privacy.

White women who choose to join are invited to the gym, a training room, where they work through a series of modules on how to be an effective ally. The aim of this required receptive reading is to teach participants how to become a better listener, recognize their White privilege, and learn how to effectively support women of colour in online and offline spaces. Those who wish to enter the training room must first make a donation to a women of colour relief fund, a charity that the group has chosen to support. Not everyone who joins the training completes it and is invited into the house, the network of the Alliance Facebook groups. They must do all of the reading and homework assignments and attend any of the required Zoom meetings with Mary. The number of White women allies is purposefully low – around 220 members.In contrast there are over 30,000 members in total in the group.

Once invited into the house, the White women enter the living room group. In this space, where all women are allowed to speak together, White members are encouraged to let the women of colour take an active and central role in the participation. This includes composing the majority of the posts. When engaging in a reply, White members are expected to read carefully, to reflect on what they have learned in their training and offer authentic support. Where White women are allowed to participate on the commenting threads, they should not dominate the discussion. Lucy, a White moderator who assists Mary, explains that entering the Alliance Group means being intentional, and knowing "I will never graduate to expert ally." Mary confirms that too much commenting on those threads raises a certain amount of suspicion. Doing the work means constantly practising and acknowledging. It is not something one can cross off their to-do list through dominating the comments.

In the living room, if a conversation gets out of hand, a White member might be called into the mending room group. This group's name is derived from a sewing room where one might mend or repair their frayed clothing. In this case it is a place for mending tears and relationships. It is the job of the moderator to call White members into the mending room to take the conversation out of the living room. When one White member is called to the mending room, all of the other White members must participate in the reckoning and healing through the discussions that unfold in the comments. Women of Colour members can, but are not required, to visit the mending room to read, observe, and listen in as a way to ensure that White moderators are effectively working with White participants to understand why their communication is offensive, hurtful, or unproductive.

Lurking is a term that the moderators consistently use in their training sessions in the gym and the healing sessions in the mending room. Around the time of George Floyd's murder, Mary recounts that "White members were not behaving well." All White members were invited into the mending room for special training. Members not willing to participate in the training were removed from the Alliance Group network. The training included discussion questions and guided objectives for how to participate and be an effective ally. In the mending room participants were told "There's no lurking. This is a working group. It is not a reading group. You do not sit back and just watch. You participate." It was made clear to members that there are spaces and times for lurking, but the mending room requires active participation.

However, required active participation does not mean daily commenting. As the group became larger there was a time around the two-year anniversary where the moderators issued a warning that they were going to purge membership. Anyone who hadn't actively commented in the last 24 months was going to be removed from the group. Members wishing not to be removed had to make their presence known. The participation that is required, however, often requires offline actions. For example, the Alliance Group supports indigenous women in the Dakotas with feminine hygiene supplies that are difficult to acquire because of their cost and the inconsistent coverage under the Supplemental Nutrition Assistance Program (SNAP) and Women Infant Child (WIC) policies.[9] Once a month, all members were required to attend a virtual event by either make a donation or tag other members to remind them to make a monetary donation. All the money collected would then go towards a bulk order from Amazon. There was no minimum donation required. Members who donated would indicate this by clicking the attending button. Members who were unable to financially contribute could participate, by tagging other members. Members are actively discouraged from commenting. The participation is limited to the binary action of donating or tagging to remind others to donate. Members are not allowed to post narratives of why they are not able to donate or contextualize why they cannot budget for this expense. The reason behind this is that, as Mary explains, "It's very painful for women of colour when White women are asked to do something really minimal, then they jump in with excuses. So we don't allow that." Commenting is more hurtful than not commenting.

Receptive reading is the first step towards activism and the moderators of the Alliance Group play a vital role in making sure that the experiences of

Black women are amplified. This means that they have to require strategic silence on the part of the members. Receptive reading, however, is not enough to become an ally. Being an ally requires a continuous commitment. If the voices of Black women are silenced, whether it is in online or offline spaces, White women must speak up to ensure that they are given the floor to speak. Mary explains, "We assume that you are doing the work outside in the real world. That's the point of the group." The collection of proof is a tricky thing as Mary points out that one should not have to quantify or show how they are being an ally but the living room can and should be a place for receptive reading. Where White women are allowed to talk, centring women of colour means to take several steps back to really listen. Mary asserts, "If someone's reading along and paying attention and they respond when we've requested them to do so [through the calls to action and the mending room] then that's fine."

There are now roughly seven moderators alongside two administrators who manage the Alliance Group. Some are retired from their professions and can devote almost 50 hours a week to moderation, while others manage moderating alongside full-time employment. There have been moderators who have chosen or have been asked to step down because they cannot keep up with the demands of moderation. What began as a US-based group has become global with members across multiple time zones in Europe and Australia.

Aside from the tremendous time commitments, Lucy, one of the other White moderators, explains that there are many challenges to active moderation. She says:

> 'First of all, we are committed to centering Black women and women of colour. That means being aware of our defensiveness and our ability to be weaponized against them. It means bearing witness to their anger without deflecting. It means truly internalizing that we are not experts on racism and they are. It means believing their lived experience without discounting or making excuses for other White people. Oftentimes, if I get pulled in, fellow White women will ignore them and only respond to me. They have this expectation that I will reinforce White supremacy with them. They go through this process of beseeching me, expressing betrayal, and lashing out. It's important not to ignore women of colour or let them be ignored.'

She feels that reading before gaining access to the network is essential: "It is so easy to make a defensive or glib comment if we aren't intentional." To keep focused and intentional, she reads and revisits Dr King's 'Six principles of non-violence' before engaging on the topic of racism. In re-reading this before moderating, she reminds herself that "Non-violent action is meant to discomfort and challenge one's moral imagination. It's easy to be snarky to bigots on our public page. The challenge we face is not getting in the way of the message. It's also not okay to appropriate anger." The attention to tone and purpose that guides her practice is one where she is thinking about both those participating on the commenting threads and those who are lurking. "My focus is never just on one person being obnoxious. We have to keep in mind that we are speaking to lurkers and we need to keep centring women of colour."

She explains that "Many posters choose to delete their interactions when we make them uncomfortable." But depending on the order of the replies, Lucy's comments might remain, leaving a digital trace for those stumbling upon the group to see how the moderators govern and determine the degree to which they would like to participate. This kind of required receptive reading encourages White members to lean away from the aesthetic personal stance and towards an efferent stance of examining their words and actions through the lens of allyship.

Health groups

Health groups have often been cited as places where lurking can be a helpful and valuable process.[10] When someone (or someone they love) receives a medical diagnosis or suspects that they may have a medical concern, health group communities are a place where they can gather information. In 2013 the Pew Research Center studied the way that adults in the United States with chronic conditions gather, share, and create health information online and offline. They found that 29 per cent of the over 3,000 participants in their study with a chronic health condition read or watched someone else's commentary or experience about health or medical issues online. This is in contrast to the 9 per cent of participants who posted or shared about their health experience.[11] Prior research has suggested that the goal in health groups is to encourage as much participation as possible to crowd-source ideas and to offer support to those who may be struggling.[12] However, findings by social psychologist Chris Fullwood et al show that lurking, that reading to understand if this community is the right place to seek information and support, has been correlated to positive outcomes.[13] Fullwood et al developed a survey for members of online health groups to explore the questions: '1) To what extent do individual reasons for lurking predict benefits or lack of benefits (e.g. empowering outcomes) that users derive from being part of an online health support group?; 2) To what extent do individual reasons for lurking predict how often users post comments and reply to others?'[14] They based their analysis on the responses of 237 participants, who had previously participated in an online health group. From these responses they were able to develop a Propensity for Online

Community Contribution Scale, which explores the relationship between nine factors:

1. poor sense of community;
2. struggles with self-expression;
3. inhibited disclosure and privacy;
4. negative online interactions;
5. ease of access and use;
6. health preventing contribution;
7. delayed and selective contribution;
8. goals met without contribution; and
9. lack of time and online health group support usage.

Of these eight factors, five of them (poor sense of community; inhibited disclosure and privacy; health preventing contribution; delayed and selective contribution; goals met without contribution) significantly predicted online health support group contribution and positive experiences in the form of empowering processes that help participants cope with illness.

The findings of this study offer important insight in how to support those coping with illness, but they also have significant implications for those interested in studying the phenomenon of lurking. The factor analysis shows that while some participants begin as lurkers and then later, as they become more comfortable with the online health group, become contributors and ultimately viewed the experience of participating in the group as empowering, others experience empowerment without ever becoming a contributor. Fullwood et al[15] (problematize the way previous psychological studies have defined the term lurker and insist that rather than looking at a binary distinction of equating no postings with lurking and at least one post with active participation, researchers should conceptualize lurking as degree of participation along a continuum of participant practices and seek to illuminate the reasons why an individual engages in those practices. Since lurking is a situation-specific behaviour employed by all users at one time or another, the researchers suggest that further ethnographic studies be completed to better understand the context for what constitutes these degrees of lurking.

Regardless of whether or not one ever becomes a consistent contributor to a health community, lurking, just reading, is valuable. This introductory period where a person is trying to make sense of their symptoms or diagnosis has been described by health researchers as sensemaking.[16] This builds upon the work by organizational psychologist Karl Weick's theory of sensemaking, which posits that organizational sensemaking can be driven by beliefs or actions of individuals within the collective organization.[17] Applying sensemaking to literacy opens up another way of understanding the value in lurking for those with health-related concerns. Due to the highly sensitive and private content shared in health groups, I used a convenience sample and asked contacts to post in the health-based Facebook groups to which they belong and invite members to participate in a brief research questionnaire and participate in a one-on-one interview about their online reading practices. The interview participants signed an IRB consent and their names have been pseudonymized. From the interviews it becomes clear that sensemaking is deeply influenced by the role of the group moderator.

Sensemaking

In terms of social media, one of the gratifications a person sought by lurking in health groups is to determine whether the symptoms they or their loved one are experiencing are unique. In health-related Facebook groups whose purpose is to support, there is a sense that the collective, even being able to see the number of people registered to the group, makes one feel less alone. As Sarah, one participant who belongs to a group for the parents of children with rare diseases explained, "So much of the health journey is lonely and isolating." Although one does not want to be, as she says, "purely extractive," reading the stories of others allows one to feel that they are a part of something, particularly when the offline alternative may not be feasible. The time-consuming nature of caring for a sick child limits the scope of one's world, particularly when much time is spent moving among various places for treatment. The online space opens up an easy place to connect. Katie O'Brien, then staff writer for the *New York Times*, expressed a similar sentiment in her op-ed 'I can't jump ship from Facebook yet', about an autism group she joined when her child was diagnosed with autism. She writes: 'I am not even that active in these groups, but it's reassuring to hear from other parents, even just online.'[18] Of course the sharing of information is what makes these groups vital, but not everyone is at a place on their journey where they are ready to share or are even knowledgeable enough about the condition to share. This aligns with previous research that people lurk because they do not have enough information to enter the conversation.

Identity formation is another gratification sought from sensemaking. Where identity formation through lurking, as discussed in Chapter 1, has been a part of LGBTQIA+ identity formation since the early days of the internet, it is also applicable to those seeking health information. Sarah explains that sometimes a complex range of symptoms make accurate diagnosis a challenge, especially for parents who rely on both what they observe and what their child can communicate. People seek out health groups as a way to confirm whether or not others have experienced similar symptoms and, if so, what diagnosis they received and how they are managing their care. Equally important is reading the posts of others to rule out or determine that your experience does not resonate with the conditions discussed in the group. Finding a connection can be an affirming experience. John, a member of an ichthyosis support group for people with a rare skin condition, says that he finds solidarity in reading the posts of others, but not commenting. In this group people share photos of parts of their afflicted bodies and since this skin condition is rare and sometimes skips one or more generations, the group might be the first time someone has seen another person who looks like them.

Another gratification sought through sensemaking is determining the relative safety of the space. There is the fear of both mediated lurking and the fear of corporate data collection. Mediated lurking, a term coined by J. T. Child, refers to the lateral surveillance of Facebook friends.[19] For example, a person choosing to view the posts of an ex-significant other without commenting or otherwise making their presence known through publicity metrics. These two people are consensually connected on the platform as friends even though their personal circumstances offline have changed.[20] Because Facebook, unlike LinkedIn for example, does not share view and hover metrics with its account holders, it is much easier to be a mediated lurker on a platform like Facebook. Sarah said that even though some of the health-related groups she is in can number in the thousands, she will occasionally see the names of people that she is acquainted with through attending the same treatment sites. This gives her pause in posting because even though she would pseudonymize her child's name and identifying information, there would be members of the group who could easily identify her child. It is a Sisyphean effort to try and hide your private information from Facebook once inside the group, but Sarah tries to limit the amount of information that can be gleaned by other members. Laine, another participant, explains that for a condition like cancer or multiple sclerosis, she might be "more circumspect," but since she is in a group for a rare genetic condition that she does not believe would alter the price of her healthcare coverage, she feels that the group is relatively safe.

Moderators play a vital role in orchestrating the participatory practices of the group. Health information technology scholar Lynette Hammond Gerrido, who studies breast cancer genetic testing decisions and racial disparities, explains that "literacy is a bridge to sensemaking, it is only one of many things that will help you make sense of something."[21] A significant number of offline actions must also take place along one's health journey. Where someone goes offline for treatment, and for support, can be influenced by what one has read in the group. The stakes are high for group members who rely on community support to help them navigate the healthcare system.

Andrea Downing, a member of a breast cancer support Facebook group, founded the Light Collective after learning that the breast cancer support Facebook group she was in had data security breaches.[22] The purpose of the Light Collective is to advocate for patient groups and to offer support to people seeking community on their healthcare journey. Light Collective, working alongside the Robin Wood Johnson Foundation, surveyed 279 members of multiple cancer-focused online groups and conducted interviews with the moderators of these groups.[23] This study found that moderators experienced a high level of burnout over the demands of the role. In this voluntary position, the need to regulate the information shared and limit the spread of medical misinformation is vital. Moreover, the burden of sharing in the grief, fear, and uncertainty that members face about their own lives can be exhausting. Moderators are often those who have survived and want to share hope or who really want to help people out of that scary and uncertain space. A person who chooses to become a moderator loses the privilege of lurking.

Neighbourhood groups

Moderators play a crucial role in determining the degree to which members of neighbourhood Facebook groups choose to use publicity metrics. The leaders of neighbourhood Facebook groups differ from other online communities in that they often live in the same geographic area as other members of the group. Therefore, the power they wield online can have local reverberations offline. Community members look to the moderator for leadership. The participants of this study signed an IRB consent form and their names have been pseudonymized (see Chapter 3 for more information on the participants). Where the participants had differing opinions on their preferred moderating style, all agreed that they were more likely to engage in publicity metrics if they supported the governing style of the moderator. Kristen said that she prefers moderators who don't "make their presence known." By this she means that there is a harmonious relationship between the moderator and members. The members know what is appropriate discourse for the group and strive to follow the norms. If they step out of line, the moderator redirects them, but ideally this is a rare occurrence. When conflicts arise between moderators and the members they govern, members look towards participatory restraint as a way to resist while maintaining offline relationships.

Participatory restraint against moderators

Mallory logged onto her neighbourhood Facebook one day and came across a post with a picture of the back of a car with its licence plate number in clear view. She paraphrased the text of the post as "Hey, whoever's car this is, your wife's having sex in there and throwing condoms out of the window and leaving them on my father's front lawn. Here's the licence plate."

She was shocked by the post: the frankness of the language and the audacity of sharing personal information without consent. What most disturbed her was that a bumper sticker for a local elementary school was on the back of the car. The licence plate and bumper sticker, coupled with the colour and make of the vehicle, were enough clues to potentially identify the owner of the vehicle. Beyond the defamation of the couple allegedly committing adultery, the link to the local elementary school presents the possibility that a child will learn of the rumours spread about their parent on Facebook.

Mallory was relieved, however, that the post was rendered in what she believes to be the better moderated Whitman Circle Facebook group. She, and several of her friends, resisted engaging in publicity metrics on the post. Offline they contacted the moderator of the group using phone and text message. Within an hour the post was removed. Had that same post been shared in another Whitman Circle group the moderator might have left it up and let the comment thread explode with jokes. Since moderating is a 24-hour-a-day, seven-day-a-week job, without compensation, it requires a high level of commitment. Moreover, because a moderator cannot turn off the group for a few hours to go to sleep or go to work, it is not possible for even the most diligent of moderators to be available to actively respond to every interaction that needs intervention.

Jessica, who moderates an Ocean Ridge neighbourhood group, has said that over the course of her almost seven years as a moderator, she has needed to set more rules and posting boundaries to ensure that she can manage the comments of over 2,000 members of the group. With assistance from another group member, she wrote a lengthy Code of Conduct covering the scope of what she, and by extension the members who elect to remain in the group, believe to be the core principles of the community. This includes striving to make the community a harassment free space. The sharing of screenshots, presumably with the intent to insult or harass, is prohibited. However, there are no tools at the moderator's disposal to verify whether or not screenshotting has occurred and for what purpose. Instead, members who feel harassed or unsafe should report the incident to her directly. There are times during the year when tensions rise around school board elections or other civic events. During these times she institutes a post moderation policy where all posts need to be approved before they are published to the community. Where this minimizes the potential chaos that could erupt in the newsfeed, members could still compose comments without approval. Therefore, these strategies alone are not enough to allow a proper respite from moderating. She can turn off her phone or choose not to receive notifications of new posts while sleeping or driving, and so on, but the group communication continues regardless of whether or not she is actively moderating. And she hopes that when she does step away that members behave themselves with decorum. Claudia, Kristen, and Shannon, in interviews conducted separately, cited Jessica's moderation style as one that made them feel supported and willing to engage. This is a sharp contrast to another Ocean Ridge neighbourhood group that they once belonged to, moderated by Charlie.

Charlie's Ocean Ridge neighbourhood group, like all of the local groups, became heated around the time of the school board elections. The school board is comprised of volunteer members of the community who are elected to establish goals, set policy, and oversee the resources for the school district. As moderator, Charlie allowed antisemitic content to be posted about a school board candidate. The post received comments from both those who found it funny alongside those who dissented the action. Charlie did not approve of anyone disagreeing with his decisions as moderator. Those who offered divergent thought would be removed from the group. For a while Claudia, Shannon, and Kristen stayed in the group to lurk because they thought that it was important to know what was being discussed. They feared that hate speech might become hateful action. Kristen even signed a petition to try and have Facebook intervene and remove the moderator. When these actions did not yield a change and the moderator continued to remove members with dissenting voices, they had an offline discussion among their respective groups of friends and came to the conclusion that their presence in the Facebook group amplified the impact of the offensive content. They left the group to lower the moderator's group numbers and reach because it was the only course of action available to them that would have an impact. Participatory restraint led them to choose to remove themselves from the audience, and thus limit the spread of antisemitic content.

Conclusion

Moderators can encourage more public contributions from group members by creating a place that is psychologically safe. They must also build community and maintain it. This means that moderators need to hold space for those who wish to publicly participate and those who do not and consider how the words and actions of those who publicly participate influence those who are mostly just reading. To achieve this, platforms need to be more actively engaged in moderation.

Facebook has begun to acknowledge the importance of lurkers although they do not refer to them as such. At the Facebook's Communities Summit, which took place on 1 October 2020, the platform announced significant changes to its online moderation tools for users. Facebook has offered a Communities Summit for Facebook moderators since 2017. It was at the 2017 Summit that Mark Zuckerberg announced that the mission of the company was changing to 'empowering people to build community and bring people closer together'.[24] This change was in response to the 2017 US

Senate hearings, which sought to determine the extent to which Facebook, among other big tech companies, was aware of international interference in the 2016 presidential elections. Since then, Facebook has invested in changes to the groups feature, shifting the emphasis to community. According to Facebook, more than 70 million group administrators are running or moderating groups worldwide and there are 1.8 billion people in groups with half of all Facebook users being members of five or more community groups.[25] One of the features that Facebook is encouraging moderators to use is Admin Assist, a tool that places a hold on group members' participation, giving them a waiting period where they can read and learn the culture of the group before engaging in vanity metrics.

It is important to note that Meta, the parent company of Facebook, Instagram, and WhatsApp, utilizes both Facebook account holders and contracted third-party content moderators to enhance the moderation capabilities of its algorithm. This differs from platforms like TikTok and X that depend mostly on the use of contracted third-party content moderators. At the time of this writing, the third-party contracted content moderators at Meta and TikTok who work in Germany have united across platforms to demand better working conditions and a fair contract.[26] Their work entails screening and possibly removing violent, sexual, and illegal content, a highly skilled process that requires cultural and language expertise. It is also a psychologically draining and difficult job to continuously view content that ranges from disturbing to horrific. They are, in essence, professional lurkers.

Outsourcing these roles to third-party companies and issuing temporary contracts relegates these incredibly important roles to the bottom of the tech industry hierarchy. Despite the challenges and expertise required, it is a low wage, low prestige, precarious position. As Sarah T. Roberts discusses in her extensive research of commercial content moderators, *Behind the Screen*, content moderators 'make increasingly sophisticated decisions and will often be asked to do so under challenging productivity metrics that demand speed, accuracy, and resiliency of spirit, even when confronted by some of humanity's worst expressions of itself'.[27] The classification of the job as unskilled, coupled with the low salary, means that international workers who are highly sought after for their language and cultural knowledge face many obstacles in acquiring and maintaining work visas. Yet without these contracted third-party content moderators, the social media monoliths would implode. The solidarity of contracted third-party moderators across platforms is a hopeful sign that if their working conditions can improve, the role of volunteer Facebook group moderators will receive more resources to effectively govern their communities.

Resistance and Refusal: (Re)Evaluating Media Literacy

In the summer of 2020, the 'I am 100% for' meme ignited contentious discussion across US-based Facebook groups.[1] The actual text of the meme reads: 'I am 100% / for mandatory / vacations / how about you?' in black coloured font. The background of the meme is composed of gentle aquamarine swirls reminiscent of ocean waves. A diagonal hypodermic needle is overlaid on the seascape background, the tip of the needle pointing into the cap of a dark red vial obscuring part of the letters a, t, i, o, and n in the word vacations. The red top of the vial also tilts at a diagonal that directs the viewer's gaze towards the word mandatory. The meme has been intentionally designed to induce the reader to miscue and to register the message of the text as 'I am 100% / for mandatory / vaccinations / how about you?'. Miscue is when the observed response of a reader does not match the expected response.[2]

The thunderous response on commenting threads was based on two key receptors. The first is the divided stance of Americans on the effectiveness and safety of the yet-to-be-authorized COVID-19 vaccines and the fear, at that time, that the United States would institute a federal vaccination requirement when the vaccines became approved and available for use. This tension was heightened by the strategic employment of visuals in the meme's design to make the text less accessible to the human eye, thus leading a great many readers to miscue the message. Those who recognized their own miscue were able to re-read the text and discern that the actual words of the meme supported a pro-vacation policy.[3] In the United States there is no federal requirement entitling workers to paid (or unpaid) employment protected vacation time. The readers who were cognisant of their miscue found themselves embroiled in debate with commenters who were unaware they were miscuing the correct reading of the meme. Some sought to contextualize their affirmation through publicity metrics. The cognisant wrote comments, for example, to explain that they liked the meme because they were in support of vacations, rather than pro-vaccinations. Therefore, the tensions that arose were about more than just the already contentious vaccine content, but over the act of miscue. Within literacy studies it has been established that all readers miscue. It is the kinds of miscues and the way one navigates them that determines whether or not one is regarded as a less efficient reader.[4] This is one of the main reasons why literacy studies scholars and practitioners prefer the term miscue over error. Though, unless one is a literacy scholar, the commonality of miscue is not readily apparent.

Miscue is instead coded as a marker of low social class and a lack of intellectual prowess. This is evidenced in the memes that circulate in response to public miscue as seen in the 'I am 100%' threads. In one example a meme depicts Gaston from Disney's *Beauty and the Beast* holding the book of the voracious reading heroine Belle upside down with the title 'How can you read this? / There's no pictures'.[5] In another, a gif of a shooting star bursts into the words 'The more you know', an allusion to the US-based National Broadcasting Company's educational public service messages of the late 20th and early 21st centuries.[6] Selecting one of these memes as a reply is an attempt to valorize the position of a certain kind of reader within a networked audience. The imaginary erudite reader is one who accurately recognizes each word on the screen and quickly comprehends the full conventional meaning of the text.

Reading in this manner is, as literacy scholar Ken Goodman writes in his book of the same name, 'a grand illusion'.[7] Eye-tracking research reveals that our eyes do not move in a consistent linear pattern across sentences clearly typed in standard sized and styled font, regardless of our degree of proficiency.[8] We regularly misidentify and misplace the letters in the words we read. This depiction of the flawless erudite reader persists in part because people who received their primary and/or secondary education in a member nation of the Organisation for Economic Co-operation and Development, which administers the Program for International Student Assessment, were likely given formal literacy instruction within a levelled reading approach.[9] Levelled reading seeks to sort people into stratified tiers of reading proficiency. It is a highly commodified educational approach and a large market of goods and services are available to serve each individual tier of reader.[10] Depending on the product purchased by the school, readers can be categorized by alphabetic or numeric tiers. Those overseeing the classroom might even choose to publicly post the literacy level of each individual student. A downstream effect of levelled reading, however, is the appropriation of the tiers into a mark of morality. Classification in the top level can be conflated with superior wisdom, judgement, and ethics.

In their research on miscue analysis, literacy scholars Yetta M. Goodman, Dorothy J. Watson, and Carolyn L. Burke describe reading across a continuum of proficient, efficient, and less efficient.[11] Their work both contrasts previous generations of scholars who labelled readers within binary distinctions of literate/illiterate and complicates the work on strict stratifications of levelled reading.[12] Goodman et al's classifications allow practitioners to examine the complex semantic, syntactic, and graphophonic cues a reader articulates while reading aloud and the meaning(s) they gather. Semantic cues refer to expressed word meaning and sentence context. Syntactic cues refer to the grammatical context. Graphophonic cues refer to visual recognition of letters and sounds. When engaging in retrospective miscue analysis of early childhood readers, for example, even less efficient readers can demonstrate profound comprehension.[13] As we see in the 'I am 100% for' meme, syntactic, semantic, and graphophonic uses of language can be weaponized in social media spaces when memes, gifs, and other digital image text purposefully use inaccessible design to force a miscue. Media literacy initiatives do not often focus on miscue or other elements of literacy studies. Yet when we focus on the act of reading while participating in an online community it becomes clear that the hostility and animosity that arises on commenting threads is more than just a response to the content. It is a guttural reaction to a hierarchical perception of acceptable language practices.

Since danah boyd's 2018 SXSW EDU keynote, 'What hath we wrought', there has been tremendous interest in re-examining media literacy and determining the best methods for teaching it. In this talk, boyd addresses how 'narrow versions of media literacy and critical thinking are being proposed as the solution to major sociocultural issues'.[14] The current contracted approach to media literacy encourages an authoritative, rather than an epistemological, perspective. Digital sources of information, whether it be specific sites, people, or news organizations, are reduced to categorizations of valid or invalid. Effectively this removes the slow and necessary work of understanding the situated historical, cultural, social, and geographic contexts from which the media emerges. As we see in the example that opens this chapter, beliefs on the efficacy of vaccinations are fuelled, in part, by a conflation of less efficient reading with stupidity. In her analysis of the efficacy of the messaging behind COVID-19 policies, anthropologist and *Financial Times* journalist Gillian Tett, explains that '[w]hat we learned in the pandemic is that medicine alone doesn't work unless you also understand the social and cultural context and the incentives shaping people'. Understanding literacy as a socially situated practice allows us to see that resistance to vaccination is not just about mistrust of medical information, it is also a resistance to the supercilious tone of the language invoked by proponents. The hierarchies embedded in immediate literacy transactions like these are rooted in a broader imperial history of literacy. This history is often obscured because media literacy initiatives and scholarship do not directly engage with literacy studies. Understanding the social and cultural context of media messages is essential to the teaching of media literacy and it should include a greater emphasis on the ways that standardized language practices invite and/or discourage visible participation. This chapter will explore two key questions. What would it look like to centre literacy in the teaching of media literacy? And how can the literacy practices of lurkers be relevant to understanding a literacy-based approach to media literacy?

Metaphoric literacy

A shortcoming of the current state of media literacy is that the term, media literacy, utilizes a metaphoric application of the word literacy. Communications scholar W. James Potter has extensively studied the uses and definitions of the term and found that there appears to be 'no consensus' among media literacy scholars as to a shared definition of media literacy.[15] Even Potter's claim that the field 'continue[s] to struggle with the question of what is Media Literacy?' is a contentious one.[16] Potter's article, 'The state of media literacy', incited a response from media literacy scholar Renee Hobbs in a subsequent edition of the *Journal of Broadcasting and Electronic Media*. Hobbs finds Potter's analysis of the state of the field to be 'disappointing' and claims that Potter 'mischaracterizes the depth and complexity of the field'.[17] This exchange in and of itself illuminates the extent of divided opinion among scholars. In Potter's most recent research, a content analysis of the more than 400 definitional elements of media literacy found in 210 articles of the *Journal of Media Literacy Education* (*JMLE*), of which Hobbs is a founding editor, this chasm persists. Potter's research reveals that media literacy definitions are not consistently applied. Despite the claims of some scholars that there is a shared agreement among the field, due in part to the global impact of the work of the National Association of Media Literacy Education (NAMLE),[18] Potter found that 'less than 38% of all citations, which means that in over 62% of all articles published in the *Journal of Media Literacy Education*, authors ignored or rejected both of these definitions'.[19] Among these *JMLE* articles, 62 per cent of authors developed their own definitions.[20]

The one place where there is consensus is that the NAMLE definition of media literacy does not centre literacy. In the earliest days of media literacy there were two US-based organizations, the Alliance for a Media Literate America (AMLA), known today as NAMLE, and the Action Coalition for Media Education (ACME). Critical media literacy scholars, Douglas Kellner and Jeff Share, have researched the histories of the two organizations. The AMLA's goal was to 'unite media literacy organizations as well as commercial media makers',[21] whereas the ACME took 'an ardent position against any type of commercial collaboration or sponsorship'.[22] Hobbs notes that 'tension between protectionist and empowerment perspectives was long part of the media literacy field (Hobbs, 1998), as scholars and educators debated whether to emphasize media literacy as an expanded conceptualization of literacy or as a means to counter the negative effects of mass media and popular culture'.[23] Those that preferred a protectionist stance wanted to 'counter the effects of mass media and popular culture', and those that preferred an empowerment stance wanted to 'expand the conceptualization of literacy'.[24] The ACME took the protectionist position, focusing on the context of media messaging by focusing on media education, rather than media literacy.[25] The AMLA viewed literacy as a more academic term and an emphasis on literacy would secure the movement as a discipline within the academy rather than a 'social movement'.[26] The AMLA pursued this avenue towards the academic professionalization of media literacy and as the organization evolved from 2006 to 2008 into the NAMLE, the emphasis changed from literate to literacy, implying a continuum, rather than a fixed state of learning.[27]

Although media literacy is a part of both mission statements and guiding principles, it is utilized in different contexts. Despite the emphasis on media education in the title of the organization, the ACME still chooses to use the word literacy in its mission statement and defines media literacy education as 'skills, knowledge, and activism', with no elaboration on these terms.[28] There is also no examination of what differentiates media education from media literacy education; both terms are used in the mission. The NAMLE's six core principles of media literacy education focus mostly on pedagogy, but the second principle offers an attempt at a definition and states that media literacy education 'expands the concept of literacy to include all forms of media (i.e., reading and writing)'.[29] The structure of the sentence seems to imply that reading and writing are examples of practices that can be applied to all forms of media. In other words, one can read about media, but one can also write original media, or write about an existing form of media. An examination of the NAMLE's Media Literacy Standards, which are aligned to federal US Common Core State Standards (CCSS), indicates that their goal is to 'expand the definition of literacy' to include 'videos, websites, games, music, radio programs, and a number of other non-print texts that students and teachers alike engage with on a daily basis' and assess comprehension using CCSS 'established for reading, writing, speaking, listening, and language'.[30] Potter is one of the rare scholars who poses the question, 'What is literacy?' in relation to media literacy.[31] He offers a detailed overview of the preeminent scholars in the field of media literacy and finds that there are three main definitions:

1. increasing skills;[32]
2. building knowledge;[33] or
3. a combination of both skills and knowledge.[34]

This lack of clarity in regard to what is meant by literacy led media literacy scholar Paul Mihailidis to describe the usage of literacy as 'broad and figurative'.[35] *The Dictionary of Cultural and Critical Theory*, in its section on literacy theory, describes media literacy as being used 'metaphorically' and in sharp contrast to how reading, writing, and orality affect an individual psychology, social organization, or cultural reproduction.[36]

Media literacy scholars, across the spectrum, do not acknowledge the field of literacy studies as a discrete academic discipline. Hobbs describes media literacy as expanding 'to include the published work of critical/cultural scholars across the disciplinary landscape of rhetoric, English education, film studies, technology education, and other fields'.[37] Mihailidis states that '[t]he most obvious location for media literacy in higher education to date has been in schools of mass communication, journalism, media studies, and education. Media literacy courses also exist less frequently in English and American studies'.[38] Indeed, literacy studies programmes are often found within schools of education; however, both Hobbs and Mihailidis explicitly identify the specific fields of rhetoric, English, and American studies without generalizing a reference to the college of liberal arts and sciences, where these kinds of programmes are usually housed. Even in more recent research, literacy studies remain absent. Bulger and Davison's report, *The Promises, Challenges, and Futures of Media Literacy*, encourages media literacy scholars and educators to improve cross-disciplinary collaboration, because '[m]edia literacy is often seen as a narrow, pedagogical field. But work from other disciplines – social psychology, political science, sociology – is producing new research and findings that could greatly benefit media literacy'.[39] The future of media literacy may look towards the general direction of the social sciences, but literacy studies should explicitly be part of that examination.

Colonizing effects of literacy

By mollifying the literacy aspects of media literacy, the field has become divorced from the colonial history of literacy as a tool of both oppression and liberation. Literacy is emancipatory. It is the process through which a person can fully participate in society and have the opportunity, in some cases, to better the circumstances into which they are born. However, literacy can also be a tool of oppression, most notably the ways in which the English language retains hegemonic influence in the global economy. Thinking about literacy as a colonizing practice is imperative to our understanding of the current state of media literacy, which 'favours standardised' ways of participation.[40] It also presents a way of conceptualizing the internet as a colonized space. Before thinking about the challenges to teaching media literacy and the role that lurkers play in the global media literacy landscape, it is necessary to first contextualize print-based literacy as both a tool of liberation and oppression.

In the standard view of literacy, the process of learning to read a printed language is one that offers the possibility of both aesthetic and efferent rewards. Reading can be a 'window to the world' as the quote attributed to novelist Lyn Butler proclaims on many an embroidered bookmark on Pinterest.[41] It is the process through which one finds joy in a primarily aesthetic stance. This aestheticization is a private experience, one that is distinct from the romantic visions of the reader that permeate popular consumer culture. Enter any still-existing Barnes & Noble, whose official corporate name no longer includes the word Booksellers, and you'll find more book-loving toys and knick-knacks than you will actual books.[42] Consumption of Virginia Woolf bobble heads and *To Kill A Mockingbird* tote bags undermines the truly radical transformative experience of aesthetic reading.

The aesthetic is vital because of the ways in which it allows an individual to imagine new possibilities that can be efferently enacted as a tool for liberation. Abolitionist Frederick Douglass writes in his memoir, 'Once you learn to read, you will be forever free'. For Douglass, a Black man born enslaved in the United States in the 19th century, reading led to a literal liberation. It was illegal for an enslaved person to possess literacy. However, he was taught the alphabet by his enslaver, Sophia Auld. Her husband, Hugh Auld, prevented Sophia Auld from furthering Douglass' education beyond alphabetic recognition. Prior to her marriage, Auld had never encountered an enslaved person. She did not fully understand that enslavers strategically withheld literacy as one of many tools of captivity. As Auld assimilated into her new role, she adopted the crueler practices of an enslaver.[43] However, the introduction of the alphabet was enough of a foundation for Douglass to autodidactically learn to read.

Reading for Douglass was an aesthetic experience that later led to efferent rewards. It offered the skillset necessary to successfully escape and later lead an abolitionist movement. With great risk, Douglas fled to the North where laws protected his autonomy, and he worked cooperatively with abolitionists to lead others to freedom. Although slavery became illegal in the United States after the Civil War of 1865, literacy laws denied Black Americans, many of whom were the descendants of enslaved people, the right to vote. These federal laws persisted until a 1970 Supreme Court case, *Oregon* v *Mitchel*, ruled literacy tests for federal elections as illegal, thus upholding the 1965 Voting Rights Act.[44] At the level of state and local government, the legal protections remain less stringent. In the 21st century there are still attempts to overturn the 1965 Voting Rights Act and to return to mandating literacy tests for voter registration.

Access to literacy remains a global human rights concern. There are many ways to measure the impact of literacy on one's life. Beyond the efferent democratic rewards there is tremendous data collected by the International Literacy Association (ILA) to support the correlation between advanced literacy levels and life expectancy, health, and income. The ILA has long tracked correlations between literacy and infant mortality. In 2022, Iceland had a literacy rate of 99 per cent and had the world's lowest infant mortality rate.[45] The same has been true in Japan since the 1990s. Higher domestic literacy rates are correlated with higher domestic gross domestic product, leading the United Nations Educational, Scientific and Cultural Organization (UNESCO) to project that 171 million fewer people would live in poverty if they had increased access to literacy.[46]

Yet despite these many essential humanitarian benefits, literacy can also be a tool of oppression as one is forced to adopt standardized communication practices and/or a new language altogether. As Caliban, the "freckled monster"[47] in Shakespeare's *The Tempest* proclaims to the Europeans who enslaved him after they were shipwrecked on the island of his birth:

> You taught me language; and my profit on 't
> Is, I know how to curse: the red plague rid you,
> For learning me your language.[48]

Caliban is a literary figure interpreted by post-colonial theorists as a representation of the way that indigenous people have long been oppressed by language.[49] As Caliban proclaims, one can understand the sophistications of a language, while also routinely denied the ability to fully participate in the political and economic system associated with that language. Post-colonial theorist Gayatri Spivak posits in *Can the Subaltern Speak?* that the suppression of language is directly tied to economic agency.[50] Through colonialism, the English language has become the dominant means of communication in diplomacy, business, entertainment, and the internet. This shifts power and agency from other global languages. Moreover, within Standard American or Standard British English, Black vernaculars, for example, utilize their own distinct grammar and usage. These variations within the English language are subjugated, forcing Black people to code switch to Standardized English in order to fully access economic and social capital. The analogy I would like to draw, and unpack in the next few paragraphs, is between standardized language practices and social media participations. To make sense of these distinctions, it is important to first begin by thinking about equitable access to the tools of communication.

In the global digital economy, creators are valued by some estimates at US$100 billion with more than 50 million people self-identifying as creators.[51] Extensive research by communications scholar Brooke Erin Duffy has shown that creators exist in a system designed to restrict their income.[52] Although many aspire to be an influencer, few will earn a living wage. This is especially true for Black Indigenous People of Color (BIPOC) creators.[53] Our current social media ecosystem operates on a game theory model of pay-to-play[54] where organic content, unlike sponsored content, is less likely to reach target audiences. To be seen in newsfeeds means that one must invest in promoted content, and even those investments often generate meagre rewards.[55] Where these economic limitations are well documented, what is less apparent is the assumed equivocal possibility of authentic participation. There is substantial research on the global digital divide between wealthy and poor communities and the methods of ameliorating this divide through the increasing equitable access to devices and further developing access points for broadband and Wi-Fi___33.[56] These products and services attempt to move people towards the possibility of digital participation through engaging in content creation and publicity metric engagement. Equitable access to communication tools is essential, but the opportunity to participate in content creation and publicity metric engagement can also be oppressive.

Lurking as privilege

Access to higher forms of literacy is a privilege. This includes lurking. To be a lurker is a privileged position. The internet is a transactional space and data is the currency. The ability to withhold some data, to resist engaging in publicity metrics is not universally accessible. Computer scientist and philosophical tech writer Jaron Lanier's book, *10 Reasons for Deleting Your Social Media Accounts Now*, offers readers a strong argument for refusing to participate in social media and robust examples of the deleterious effects of a social media presence.[57] Although written in 2018, its points have only become more prescient in recent years. Lanier recognizes that many people rely on social media for their livelihood. In a podcast interview for *The Sway* with the *New York Times*' Kara Swisher, he concedes that some people may not be able to leave social media, but that the number is probably quite small.[58] He says:

> If you are actually in a position to quit and you don't, you're making yourself part of the problem. You're not doing anything to free those who are more trapped. You're only enslaving them more by entrenching the system. As an affluent or valuable person to the system, you're the one that the whole system is being funded by.[59]

Where Lanier is cognisant that it is the affluent exploiting those with lower socioeconomic status, his words assume that the people who largely use social media are affluent, like himself. Taken as a polemic, a text purposefully designed to posit an extreme position to generate healthy debate and an interrogation of values, Lanier's text is important. The degree to which his suggestions can be executed depend on a person's socioeconomic position, which is often influenced by other sociological constructs of race, ethnicity, gender, sexual orientation, and so on.

For example, he suggests that those who work in media industries be creative and make use of public offline events in metropolitan areas like San Francisco and New York City to generate publicity. This American-centric view assumes that everyone participating in the media industry along the spectrum from creator to consumer does so from a US metropole. Media industry professionals in these cities are often White and 'legacied', meaning that they are the descendant of someone who is already considered a media elite.[60] Moreover he states that he does not use social media to promote his books and that they do 'just fine'. Although he doesn't specify how much income generated from his books allows him to exist 'just fine', it is worth noting that Lanier's affluence comes not from being a writer, but for his work as a computer scientist, noted as being one of the founders of Virtual Reality. For an author relying on their income primarily from writing endeavours, one would not likely be able to be 'just fine' without social media promotion by someone. Even if one could avoid social media use entirely, the promotional labour is then outsourced to other professionals or to the fans themselves.[61]

By extension, if few can actually delete all of their social media accounts, resisting social media usage has a direct impact on local BIPOC economies. The presumed person using social media continues to be White and affluent. André Brock, an interdisciplinary scholar of race representations in social media, explains that 'online identity has long been conflated with whiteness, even as whiteness is itself signified as universal, raceless, technocultural identity'.[62] To be a lurker is an increasingly privileged position. The colonization of internet spaces by corporate entities heightens the cost of privacy. In the conclusion of Safiya Umoja Noble's *Algorithms of Oppression*, she shares the story of Kandis, a Black beauty shop owner, who narrates how unethical algorithmic bias effects search results through Yelp erased her local business from potential customers. Kandis had a thriving beauty shop business that began to suffer because her clients were not actively reviewing her business on Yelp. 'The internet/Yelp told people I did not exist. I think algorithms don't take into consideration communities of color and their culture of trusting in the web with our personal information out like that. And just because I don't have reviews doesn't mean that I have no value.'[63] Through this narrative account, we see how resistance to social media participation disproportionately impacts BIPOC-owned businesses and the people whose livelihoods depend on those businesses.

Examining media literacy education from a literacy studies perspective presents three key challenges. The first is the Anglocentric nature of the field, the attenuated focus on youth populations, and the emphasis on acts of public participation. The next section will discuss ways to confront those challenges.

Confronting global challenges to media literacy

It is important to first address where in the world formal media literacy policies and initiatives are enacted. The most robust and detailed policies can be found in the United States, Canada, New Zealand, the United Kingdom, Australia, and the European Union. The next few sections will unpack some of the limitations of what is offered, but in terms of policy development and initiatives, these nations and regions are at the vanguard.

The Communication and Media Research Institute at the University of Westminster studied the media literacy and misinformation policies in seven sub-Saharan African nations and found that the teaching of media literacy was only enacted in one province in South Africa.[64] In all other areas within the scope of their study, it was not a part of the national curriculum. Notably in the Western Cape province of South Africa, one of the wealthiest provinces in the country, 'click restraint' was one of the topics taught. The other countries studied – Cote d'Ivoire, Ghana, Kenya, Nigeria, Senegal, and Uganda – offered curriculum with computing skills as opposed to media literacy. The English language itself provides additional hurdles to effectively teaching media literacy. In Nigeria, for example, there are five nationally recognized languages and more than 500 vernaculars.[65] Approximately 60 per cent of the nation is functionally literate in English and the media and journalism is primarily composed in English.[66] Therefore, approaches to teaching any form of media literacy miss at least 40 per cent of the population.

In Latin America, national initiatives for media literacy, where they exist, mostly focus on skill development.[67] Peru and Mexico, for example, teach search and digital competencies, but do not make the larger connection to media literacy.[68] Argentina is a rare exception and has a more robust nationalized media literacy programme that focuses on media production and an analysis of media messaging.[69] Likewise in Asia, India stands out for its initiatives scattered across some, but not all, provinces, again centring more on production than interpreting messaging.[70] Japan, too, has one of the more robust media literacy initiatives in the region.[71] Whereas East and Southeast Asian nations, such as Singapore, Malaysia, and Thailand, have stricter government control of media and thus authentic media literacy is a challenge.[72] In Russia, nationalized media literacy policies do not exist.[73] Where Anglocentric media literacy initiatives offer more than what can be found in many other parts of the world, these initiatives focus primarily on teaching children and adolescents. Furthermore, the content taught does not often include acts of private participation.

Continued emphasis on youth

There are essentially two nationalized approaches to media literacy:

1. a not-for-profit alliance model; and
2. a nationalized government-funded initiative.

The United States, Canada, and New Zealand operate under the former. In the United States there are several not-for-profit organizations that work together under the heading of the National Media Literacy Alliance (NMLA). The mission statements of the partner organizations in the NMLA exclusively focus on education in the primary and secondary education sectors. All of the partner organizations that comprise the alliance direct their efforts towards working with teachers and parents who are self-motivated to locate these resources. There is not a concerted effort to work with the larger population beyond those affiliated with schools in the primary, secondary, and, to a lesser extent, higher education sectors. The NMLA does include media and library organizations like the Public Broadcasting Service; however, only the education arm of these organizations is involved with the alliance. The NAMLE, the umbrella organization for the NMLA, allows any individual free membership and allows access to their newsletter and peer-reviewed *JMLE*.[74] However, the specific implementation of media literacy initiatives is not under their purview. To be enacted these initiatives must be aligned to the national US Common Core curriculum. The Common Core curriculum is organized into two disparate academic fields: English Language Arts/Literacy and Mathematics.

The NMLA views media literacy as an endeavour shared among an interdisciplinary range of educators, not just those, like English teachers, who are typically responsible for teaching reading. The emphasis on including mathematics and science teachers, among others, is significant because it broadens the responsibility. Partner organizations like the National Council of Teachers of English (NCTE) and the National Council of Teachers of Mathematics (NCTM) are run by and serve the needs of teachers, but they do not directly control the development of national standards and policies to which schools must adhere. Membership in the NCTE and NCTM, and so on, is not compulsory for all teachers in the United States. Rather teachers can choose to pay to join these organizations or avail themselves of some of the free online resources these organizations provide. However, the conferences and the academic literature produced by most of the partner organizations are exclusively available to those who pay the membership and conference fees, fees that cash-strapped public schools are not often likely to reimburse or outright fund for teachers. Although it varies by region, when looking at national US data, teaching is one of the lowest paid professions and the onus lies firmly on each teacher's individual shoulders whether or not they can afford to invest in their own professional development for media literacy.[75]

Similarly in Canada, Media Smarts, the Centre for Digital and Media Literacy, is a not-for-profit organization that exclusively works with the primary and secondary education sector. Their mission states: 'Through our work we support adults with information and tools so they can help children and teens develop the critical thinking skills they need for interacting with the media they love.'[76] From this viewpoint, adults are the medium through which children and adolescents receive information. Adults, who might also be in need of media literacy strategies while pursuing their own media and digital content, are beyond the scope of the Media Smarts alliance. There is not, at the time of this writing, a comparable media literacy initiative targeted to adults from either an alliance or the Canadian government. An article posted by Media Smarts titled 'Why teach media literacy?' suggests that young adults will be media literate and require no further outreach if effectively taught media literacy beginning in early childhood. There is no recognition that technologies are ever evolving and continuously creating new literacies as people, of all ages, interact with them. Educational autonomy in Canada resides with the provinces. With the exception of Ontario, Canadian provinces have not yet prioritized media literacy. Part of the challenges in the North American model is the regionalized autonomy of the education sector and the lack of federal power to enact a comprehensive plan.

In New Zealand, the guiding curriculum for media literacy is nationalized in the sense that it is put forth by the National Library of New Zealand, which is funded by the New Zealand government. The mission of the New Zealand Curriculum targets young people and uses school librarians as the conduit through which to implement school-wide digital literacy programmes. Again, this emphasis on school librarians, rather than local library branches, limits the possibility of interacting with other key adult demographics.

In other parts of Oceania, there are efforts underway to expand access to media literacy education. Australian education operates on a more centralized federal model and thus has been able to move more effectively towards inclusive standards for all populations. The mission of the Australia Media Literacy Alliance (AMLA) centres on all citizens. It does not consider children and adolescents to be more vulnerable than adults when it comes to recognizing misinformation. The mission of the Australian alliance offers a three-pronged approach to teaching media literacy for all in society. The AMLA aims to:

1. articulate the achievements and challenges in the Australian context;
2. provide direction for educators and curriculum development; and
3. raise awareness and encourage a whole-of-community response.[77]

The Australian model offers more formalized collaborations with higher education, including collaborating with Queensland University of Technology and Western Sydney University to produce research that impacts federal policy. A survey of 3,510 Australian adults led by Tanya Notely, University of Western Sydney and Michael Dezuanni, Queensland University of Technology found that the expansion of media literacy initiatives beyond primary and secondary schooling is essential.[78] A national strategy to carry out these laudable goals in Australia is still in development.[79]

Nor does a media literacy strategy for adults exist in Europe. The European Union's mission for a Digital Decade encourages member states to increase access, ease digital divides and scale the digital economies, leaving the development of media literacy initiatives up to individual states. At the UNESCO Institute for Lifelong Learning, the German Federal Minister of Education, Bettina Stark-Watzinger, laments that in 2022 there is still not a comprehensive plan for media literacy education for adults in Germany.[80] The United Kingdom has recently begun to look beyond the primary and secondary sector. The United Kingdom utilizes an alliance approach to the Department for Digital, Culture, Media, and Sport develops national policies to shape media literacy education. Although it began as an outreach programme to primary and secondary schools, the Department for Digital, Culture, Media, and Sport is beginning to expand its efforts to engage with the wider population. This includes a recently launched grant programme targeting hard to access populations, specifically looking to serve adults. These programmes are still in the early stages of development at the time of this book's writing.

The lessons we can learn from studying a broader range of participation that includes lurker literacies should not be limited to primary, secondary, and higher education audiences. It must also include non-school-age populations. Media literacy alliances in North America and Oceania sponsor one media literacy week per year. This is an initiative designed to encourage nationwide school participation, without which individual states and provinces might not consciously seek to integrate their curriculum with alliance-fostered initiatives. Although these weeks focus on children and adolescents, they offer the possibility of cross-educational inclusion because workshops are offered beyond school settings and include free virtual workshops offered to parents. Through teaching parents how to help their children, the parents themselves are also learning skills that will be applicable to their own lives.

But what about adults who are not necessarily parents of school-aged children? Community-based media literacy initiatives must also take place outside of school settings and school-based affiliations. Ladan Mohammad Siad is part of a team that runs community-based media literacy workshops in Toronto and New York City, which offer BIPOC participants the opportunity to learn media literacy practices of refusal as media literacy and survival. The workshops have been hosted by both local community centres and major art museums like the New Museum in New York City and the Museum of Contemporary Art in Toronto. Siad roots contemporary social media refusal in the long history of government sponsored surveillance endured by BIPOC people from the slave registers that recorded the trafficking of Black bodies to the Indian Land Act (Canada) and the Indian Reorganization Act (United States) which continue to regulate the lives of indigenous peoples. Indigenous Services Canada and the Bureau of Indian Affairs in the United States reserves the right to recognize tribes and by extension to grant individuals affiliated with recognized tribes access to social welfare services. To obtain recognition involves the collection of detailed personal information.

Siad acknowledges the fear and trauma that participants have experienced in the process of forced sharing. Refusal involves taking control of your data footprint and identifying which parts of participation are truly optional to make choices about when and how to limit participation. Where this discussion begins with practical tips on how to control the settings on the most frequently used social media platforms among the participants, it extends towards unlearning standardized language and education practices, which constrain participation. Citing the example of the Metaverse, Siad explains that participants will say 'Mark Zuckerberg controls the Metaverse'.[81] Instead, Siad wants them to understand that the Metaverse is infinite. Zuckerberg controls a space that he will 'charge you to go into' (by charge Siad is referring to exchanges of both data and/or money). In other words, the internet is a geography. Individuals like Zuckerberg have colonized digital spaces, much in the same ways as empires and nation-states have developed. We exist within those spaces and are governed by their rules.

Siad explains that the benefits of lurking are reserved for those who have the power to withhold the data within their control, people who are White and affluent. Furthermore, Siad firmly believes that technological spaces deserve to be a public access right, in part because under the current structure, BIPOC 'are not allowed to be a lurker. You have to be either actively participating or actively ignored.'[82] This is analogous to the welfare state in that in order to receive resources, such as food and subsidized housing, one must offer the government accurate biographical and occupational information. Without this forced exchange, one is denied the resources one needs to survive. Despite these inequities, Siad believes that within these colonized internet spaces there is also a way to play and resist fear by participating in non-standardized literacy practices.

Refusal can happen within, even while an individual engages in, public acts of participation. Part of understanding play is looking towards non-standardized language practices like coded participation on Black Twitter and being AFK (away from the keyboard), a term complicated by curator and writer Legacy Russell's *Glitch Feminism* manifesto.[83] In response to social media theorist Nathan Jurgenson's advocacy of the term AFK over IRL (in real life) to signify the continuous thread between the online and offline worlds, Russell posits that AFK signifies 'a more continuous progression of the self, one that does not end when a user steps away from the computer, but rather moves forward out into society'.[84]

Public participation centred

Media literacy initiatives should move beyond their exclusive focus on public acts of participation. The NAMLE, the US non-profit that organizes the NMLA alliance, tracks the development of state standards and notes that there is not yet a national standard for media literacy practice adoption. This is in part because in the United States, educational policy is regulated by individual states. In the United States there are federal Common Core Standards that are mandated nationwide, but each individual state has localized control over implementation and interpretation of those standards. The NAMLE looks toward teachers of English Language Arts as the best medium to convey awareness because the federal Common Core Standards in English Language Arts includes the 'analysis, digital creation, and the use of non-print texts'.[85] This standard is one that refers to a student's production of digital content in lieu of traditional English Language Arts compositions and/or a student's analysis of digital content in place of novels and other print-based literature. The intent is to broaden the acceptable range of texts that one can study and compose in a primary or secondary school setting. As danah boyd asserts in her SXSW EDU keynote:

> 'Every day, I watch teenagers produce anti-Semitic and misogynistic content using the same tools that activists use to combat prejudice. It's notable that many of those who are espousing extreme viewpoints are extraordinarily skilled at using media. Today's neo-Nazis are a digital propaganda machine. Developing media making skills doesn't guarantee that someone will use them for good.'[86]

The development of the Common Core Standards, including, but not limited to, those that make reference to digital content, are scripted to easily yield towards the assessment of students and their teachers. Assessment being the necessary vehicle for justifying the allocation of federal and state funds for public education. Therefore, to qualify for operational funds, schools must demonstrate their efficacy through assessment. The collection of data for assessment typically relies on either test scores or the production of tangible classroom artefacts. Class discussions, for example, while pedagogically sound and personally meaningful, are less likely to be utilized as an assessment artefact than the creation of an essay or a blog. The funding apparatus of standards-based public education means that the intangible, yet vital, components of learning are on the periphery of the curriculum. This is a great challenge to the necessary teaching of lurker literacies and other less visible forms of digital participation. Furthermore, the Common Core Standards are written with the scope of the classroom in mind where there is a teacher to act as a moderator who can both intervene and guide discussion. On the internet the lack of active moderation from platforms, from group leaders, from nations unable to regulate content and activity, means that the Language Arts classroom does not provide the most effective model for practising this kind of media literacy.

Instead, many global media literacy curriculums focus on content creation. In the Canadian province of Ontario, there is emphasis on teaching primary and secondary students to develop a personal brand[87] as part of the official curriculum. In New Zealand it is about finding, collecting, and making content.[88]

To add to this conversation, there are two key ways to centre literacy in the teaching of media literacy and introduce a continuum of participation that includes lurker literacies. The first is to develop more inclusive media literacy standards at the national level and the second is to expand community-based educational opportunities alongside the traditional primary, secondary, and higher education sectors.

Inclusive standards

Drafting federal standards, particularly in places like the United States and Canada, where states and provinces retain a prominent degree of educational autonomy, is often Sisyphean. In spite of these challenges, it is imperative to begin to write standards that emphasize the importance of reading and strategically resisting and refusing front-facing metrics of participation. This means that more time in the classroom must be allocated towards a humanities approach to social media. In addition to teaching pause as a means to identify misleading information and verify content, teaching pause must also include an investigation of one's efferent and aesthetic purposes. In other words, we need to first determine who we are in the audience. Therefore, we need to consider:

1. Who do I want to be in this space?
2. What can I contribute within it?
3. What can I contribute beyond it?

These are questions that rely on the humanities and the liberal arts as much as they do technological acumen. It is through class discussion that understanding and reflecting on purposive pause can best be achieved. As we consider the best practices for including lurker literacies, it is important to remember that in Mike Caufield's SIFT method, the first and most important step is to stop.[89] The slowing down of our participation is necessary to limit the spread of misinformation, but it is also a place where we need to encourage time to reflect and consider our motivations. Stopping and remaining silent can be a powerful gesture. Educators need to be authorized to devote significant class time towards introspection and philosophical discussion.

As nations adopt media literacy goals or benchmarks it is imperative to include standards that reflect a continuum of participation that explicitly includes social media resistance and refusal. To teach receptive reading means to purposefully widen the range of diverse voices we follow and read content from. This must operate in tandem with specific teaching about algorithmic search bias. One of the key literacy practices of receptive reading is that people seek to verify information from both online and offline sources. Understanding how the silos of search guide us towards content is particularly important for those voracious readers engaging in strategic silences. To reach reflexive entertainment means to rigorously investigate when laughter becomes weaponized. Students need the rhetorical skills to read and comprehend content in relation to Poe's Law, which expresses the challenges of identifying an extremist view from a parody of an extreme view. Entertainment is consistently found to be a gratification sought from social media.[90] Standards must assume that students (just like their teachers) turn to social media to read for entertainment. Therefore, class discussions must centre social media reading and make visible that unlike reading offline texts, there is no such thing as 'just reading', an allusion to the Michael Jackson meme in Chapter 1.

To teach reflexive entertainment means to be reflective of the context for the production and consumption of entertaining content. Students should reflect on these questions when they turn to social media for entertainment:

1. Am I here for a laugh? If so, what makes this funny?
2. Who is hurt by my laughter?
3. Who profits from my presence in this space?

To teach sensemaking means to be goal driven when gathering information and to consider the ways one's identity formation is monitored while collecting that information. Students should reflect on these questions when they turn to social media to gather information:

1. Am I here to learn? If so, what do I intend to do with what I have learned?
2. Is this platform, community, or online space the right forum to respond?

To teach participatory restraint means to consider the effects of amplifying the message within your local and global community. Student should reflect on this question when they are moved to comment, react, or share posts on social media:

1. What are the benefits of withholding engagement?

To teach protective curation means to consider how withholding engagement can preserve community relationships. Students should reflect on these questions when they are considering withholding engagement:

1. What are the drawbacks of withholding engagement?
2. What are some of the offline ways to offer support?

Conclusion

Inclusive standards around purposive pause and community-based media literacy education are not a panacea. They are simply ways to insert lurker literacies into the pre-existing media literacy ecosystem. All educational standards and systems can be gamed for evil purposes. Paradoxically, learning how to become a proficient reader will enhance access to a higher quality of life, while simultaneously heightening access to the tools one would need to destroy that access for others. One can become a proficient reader, ascend to great political heights, and then wage unprovoked war. One can become a proficient reader, mastering media literacy education and purposive pause, and decisively spread misinformation to destabilize economies and undermine democratic principles. This is not what we immediately think about when we buy a lacy 'Reading is a window to the world' embroidered pillow: access to that world includes the possibility of engaging in greedy, mischievous, and violent interactions.

Centring literacy in the teaching of media literacy redirects the scholarly conversation towards a wider range of audience participation. This requires understanding reading as an integral part of the participatory process for people of all ages, regardless of whether or not they are affiliated with school settings. Leaders of the not-for-profit media literacy alliances and policy makers for federally sanctioned media literacy programmes should be cognisant of the vaulted position of the English language. The limitations of the totalizing impact of the English language not only restricts population access, it also presupposes a standardized approach to participation. Including lurker literacies in the teaching of media literacy is not a panacea for antagonistic behaviour, but it offers learners the opportunity to reimagine their role as digital citizens.

6

How Do We Account for Lurking? Implications for Social Science Researchers

Trying to engage lurkers can be an exhausting task. It requires patience, persistence, and a deep understanding of how to design a research project where so-called passive participation can be made visible. The 'Hey, lurkers' meme from the 'See nobody cares' collection[1] satirizes the plight of researchers attempting to recruit lurkers to participate in their research studies. The meme features a screengrab from the movie *Jurassic Park*[2] that, when contextualized within the narrative of the film, offers an apt allusion to the underlying concerns that make data collection on lurking a challenge. In *Jurassic Park*, antagonist Dr Lewis Dodgson is an academic researcher who engages in unethical research methods such as paying Jurassic Park's computer programmer Dennis Nedry to steal dinosaur embryos for the private corporation BioSyn.[3] In Michael Crichton's book, from which the film is adapted, Dodgson's character has a history of engaging in unethical studies, including testing a rabies vaccine on Chilean farmers that results in the death of at least ten uninformed participants. The meme displays a scene from the movie where Nedry and Dodgson sit in a cafe to discuss their plan to engage in unethical and criminal research methods. This is the archetype that a great many people envision when a researcher enters an online community. The internet researcher is perceived as the selfish free-rider who takes from online communities for their own profit and contributes nothing in return to the participants or the community at large.[4] Ironically, this is the same concern that internet researchers have historically felt about lurkers.[5] The distrust online community members feel for researchers is one of the reasons why it is difficult to gain their consent for studies.

For this reason, open calls or requests for lurking participants are often unanswered. In the satirical two-panelled meme, the title of the top meme reads 'Hey, lurkers we got someone who wants to chat'. In the image,

Dodgson and Nedry sit together at a table. Dodgson attempts a rather conspicuous disguise of sunglasses and an oversized hat, where Nedry, with his face fully exposed, wears a brightly coloured and loudly printed Hawaiian style shirt. Nedry points towards Dodgson with both hands and looks over his shoulder to the other patrons of the cafe. The cafe patrons remain ambivalent and do not respond to Nedry's gestures. The image in the bottom panel crops out the cafe patrons and features a close up of Dodgson and Nedry with the caption, 'See they don't care'. This represents the two approaches researchers often take to gathering data on lurking. Whether it's Dodgson's attempts at clandestine observation or Nedry's style of overt and outlandish gestures utilizing publicity metrics, both are often publicly met with silence. However, this public silence is not synonymous with an unwillingness to consent to participation.

So, how do we, as Katz once, now famously, asked, 'lure the lurkers?'[6] To successfully capture the data of lurking participants[7] there are two kinds of research questions this chapter will address. The first is research questions specifically aimed at studying lurking (or some variation on the concept of passive participation). The second are research questions on a non-lurking related topic that seeks to gather inclusive data from online communities. Where the former is specifically looking to connect with lurkers, the latter might not be aware that lurkers are missing from the study. Oftentimes studies of online communities will include a slight nod to the difficulty of recruiting lurkers or an acknowledgement that the study was not able to include lurkers in the limitations sections of the research. This is an important first step towards transparent research. To extend this gesture, this chapter will offer ways for the researcher to make an earnest attempt at reaching the other 90 per cent of community participants. There are three key questions researchers must consider in their research design:

1. How can we account for lurking in our research?
2. How do we ethically engage lurkers in our research?
3. What are the implications if we avoid lurkers?

Accounting for lurkers

Contemporary social science researchers face many compounding challenges in their work: limited access to funds; overreliance on the precarity of graduate student and contingent faculty labour; and increased institutional committee commitments that compete with research demands. These time-intensive hurdles can make it difficult to prioritize inclusive data collection methods. The most accessible data to gather from social media is that which is publicly front facing. Moving beyond the collection of publicity metrics is not an easy task when time and resources are scarce. Inclusivity in this instance is two-fold. It means the collection of data that will capture both so-called passive and active participants. It can also refer to the diversity of the subjects participating in the study. To begin, we will look at data collection methods that capture a broader range of participation. In order to do this effectively, we must think of lurkers as readers and look towards methodologies that explicate the reading process.

Quantifying passive participation

Hover metrics, page views, click-rate to response micro-metrics are quantitative ways to begin to measure and understand lurking patterns, behaviours, and gratifications. Accessing the platform's data metrics can be difficult because they are often proprietary to the platform. Furthermore, the way these metrics are designed, they are measuring presence rather than the depth and comprehension of the reading that the person pursued while lurking. For example, prior to its transformation to X, if you share an article on Twitter before clicking on the link, Twitter will ask 'Headlines don't tell the whole story. Want to read this before retweeting it?'[8] This is an attempt by the platform to minimize the spread of misinformation and an attempt to hold people accountable for their sharing behaviour through a rhetorically moralizing question. Clicking on the link to open the article is enough to satisfy the Twitter platform that the article has been read.[9] Therefore if one was able to gain official access to click-rate to response metrics on Twitter (which Twitter once defined as reading), this will not, on its own, allow us to determine the decoding and meaning-making processes of reading. After one has opened the link, the platform can track the places on the page where a finger or trackpad hovers, but this gesturing is divorced from where the eyes meet the page. Hovering does not mean that the reader's eyes have attempted to scan some or all of the words. A way to measure engagement is to study eye movement, which is one method literacy scholars employ to understand the continuum between proficient and less efficient reading practices.

Eye-tracking cameras have long been used in literacy studies to follow a reader's eyes across the page.[10] In the late 19th century, French ophthalmologist Louis Émile Javal studied eye movement in pursuit of treatments for strabismus, a vision disorder where the eyes become misaligned when looking at an object.[11] Although his research inquiries were motivated by oculomotor function and not in the science of reading, his work introduces the term saccade, which refers to the backward and forward movements an eye travels when reading. These observations on saccade were further explored by Ewald Ering and M. Lamare in relation to word recognition and comprehension. Their measurements of eye movements utilizing afterimages revealed that eyes do not smoothly move across a page.[12]

More invasive techniques were developed in the early 20th century under Edmund B. Huey who utilized a primitive contact lens with an attached pointer to track with greater precision which words a reader's eye paused upon.[13] By the 1930s Charles H. Judd had developed a non-invasive eye-tracking device, which recorded eye movements on film. From this point forward, eye-tracking cameras have been utilized by literacy scholars as a way to assess how proficient adult readers made sense of text. Although they were developed for scholarly research in reading, eye-tracking cameras have since been adopted for behavioural research and visual content analysis. Their interdisciplinary use extends beyond academia and they have been used by the gaming industry to inform decisions on game design, and in driver education programmes administered by insurance agencies to minimize traffic accidents.[14] Financial considerations have, until recently, stalled the scalability of eye-tracking research. With some high-end models currently priced at over US$10,000, their use is often limited to researchers with access to well-funded labs. Eye-tracking cameras are typically used on desktop computers that require the purchase of additional hardware; however, the last few years have seen an increase in accessible mobile technologies to measure eye movement priced below US$1,000. This is a promising development for broadening access of these tools for researchers studying lurking specifically or more comprehensive digital participation.

A cornerstone of eye-tracking research within literacy studies is the disruption of the idea that the eye of a proficient reader moves 'smoothly', left to right, across each sentence on the page. Reading utilizes ballistic eye movements. This begins with a point of fixation where the eye stabilizes on a viewing location, followed by saccade, a shift to a new viewing location that can be either forward or backward within the text. Skilled readers spend 200–250 milliseconds in the fixation position while silently reading.[15] Meaningful text processing is defined by the perceptual span and for proficient readers this means that they gather their meaning from the 14–15 characters to the right of fixation and 3–4 characters to the left of fixation.[16] Less efficient readers will have a narrower perceptual span, gathering information from fewer characters on either side.[17] During saccade, the eye scans forward and backward from the point of fixation, which allows time for the reader to process the information acquired during fixation. However, no new information is acquired during the saccade. Meaning is only created during fixation; saccade is a time for processing.

It is important to note that the majority of eye-tracking research over the past century has been performed on English-speaking adults using desktop-style screens.[18] This is significant for several reasons. The first is that proficient eye movements for processing the English language cannot and should not be universally applied to all languages. English language reading research assumes that sentences are constructed to be read left to right, whereas Arabic, Hebrew, Persian, and Urdu, for example, are read right to left. Studies performed on adults, most of whom were taught to read in a homogeneously print-centric environment prior to the advent of widespread digital screens, do not necessarily have the same eye movements as young adults and children who were taught to read using heterogeneous methods of print and digitally interactive pages. Furthermore, the large desktop screens that were used to administer these foundational research projects do not currently represent the medium in which most people engage with digital content. Laptop screens, tablets, phones, and watches offer much smaller screens with a restricted space for the eye to move within and a potentially narrower perceptual span.

Measuring where the eyes move on the screen can assist internet researchers in understanding the level of engagement and on-platform participation one pursues while lurking. Currently, eye-tracking cameras can pinpoint the exact locations where the participant gazes upon the screen, which in turn can be quantified to determine fixation and saccade. From this information alone, researchers can begin to observe with greater specificity than the platforms themselves, where a reader places their attention. This kind of research broadens our understanding of what Takashi refers to as active lurkers and what Ellison refers to as the 'non-click' when a reader hovers, but does not click, on a link.[19] The necessary addition that studies of print-based fixation and saccade can offer to internet researchers is a way to measure the proficiency of the reader. Understanding the speed and direction in which the eye moves gives a baseline for the degree to which the reader struggles with word recognition and comprehension. Researchers cannot assume that all participants are proficient readers and where demographic information might be correlated with proficient reading (high income or socioeconomic status, for example), comprehension is specific to the individual. This is vital information for those interested in studying the spread of misinformation/ disinformation and other critical media literacies. It is a useful addition to medical and psychological studies that seek to explore how lurkers comprehend the medical information they encounter in medical forums and groups. Organizational, marketing, and business researchers would find this a useful way to study the degree to which targeted marketing is understood by those who hover and do not follow through with a click to sale. Where eye cameras offer access to quantifiable data, to understand the full context of a reader's comprehension and decision-making process, it is necessary to talk to readers about their lurking.

Surveys

Studies of lurking often use surveys to recruit participants. When posting with a link to a survey hosted off-platform, potential participants need not use platform-based publicity metrics to participate. This can be enticing to people who would prefer to engage in private participation. It is also important to consider that people engaging in lurking might do so because they are reading deeply and intentionally or because they are casually scrolling and meandering about the platform. Therefore, survey design should clearly include the projected length of time to complete the survey.

Community mapping

Community mapping, sometimes referred to as asset mapping, comes from the field of education. Using community mapping is a way to anonymously crowd-source information. It has many of the same benefits of a survey; however, it also allows participants to see the responses of others participating in the survey and the opportunity to contribute new information.

Interviews

Interviews are one of the methods most needed in better understanding lurker literacies. Retrospective miscue analysis (RMA) relies, in part, on observing a reader while they are reading aloud and marking the miscues uttered as well as the corrections one might make. Further studies might include RMA as part of the interview process to understand where in the reading process the reader loses interest or becomes confused. Effectively broadening the participant demographics beyond White heteronormative participants requires a diverse research team to conduct interviews. To successfully conduct larger scale research, it is imperative that research labs be composed of a diverse group of social scientists. Beyond the socially just reasons for inclusivity, in a study of nine million papers written by six million scientists, Bedoor K. AlShebli et al found that 'papers written by ethnically diverse groups were cited 11.2% more than were papers written by non-diverse groups'.[20]

Ethically engaging lurkers

Lurkers are people

The subtitle to Joanne McNeil's book, *Lurking*, is *How a Person Became a User*. In her book, McNeil explores how the all-consuming nature of the internet has turned us into users, both in the sense of our addiction to the affordances the internet provides, but also in the way that the internet has reified us. She writes:

> Here is where users get used: as scrap metal, as data in a data set, as something less than human, as actual tools. Priceless experience, lived

online, can be boiled down to a price, which tends to be fractions of pennies. ... [B]oundaries do not always exist in academia or the media, and are definitely not the custom of Google or Facebook.[21]

The choice of the word "user" is an interesting premise and an important metaphor to explore. However, one of the problems with metaphorical thinking is that it negates the humanity of the participant. Throughout this book I have endeavoured to avoid the word 'user' to describe participants. This was at times linguistically challenging, but the overall effect dignifies the person who chooses to participate in social media activity. Shifting away from the word user in recruitment materials and in the write up of the study encourages researchers to remember the humanity o the participants. Furthermore, transparency and visibility is paramount; it is necessary to make your role as a researcher and your intentions visible to the group.

Consent: recruiting, not luring

Securing the informed consent of lurkers is perhaps the most daunting challenge to research design. Understanding that lurking is a participatory act that all people engage in from time to time should lighten that burden. Additionally, a researcher's mindset needs to shift from luring to recruiting. A person who lurks is not necessarily someone resistant to participation in academic research as evidenced by the numerous studies by Nonnecke, Preese, Honeychurch, and others that have successfully recruited lurkers.[22] People do not consistently lurk across all social media platforms. Therefore, recruiting participants across multiple platforms expands not only the range of participants, but also offers opportunities to connect with people who might be vociferous and leave a trove of publicly facing participatory data in one community while also primarily lurking in another. Limiting recruitment to only one platform also reproduces certain demographic redundancies where, for example, women with higher levels of education are most likely to use and respond to health-based inquiries on Facebook and Twitter.[23] Whereas men are more likely to use and respond to health-based inquiries on Reddit.[24]

Although lurking is a common practice, the negative and predatory connotations associated with the word are a hindrance in the recruitment effort. Where one might be self-aware that they read more than they post, or listen more than they speak, they might not wish to identify with the term lurker. In crafting a call for research participants to specifically study those who lurk, consider removing the words lurker and lurking from the initial call. It is imperative to include the following strategies for working with hard-to-reach populations. When working with difficult to access populations a more generalized call for participants lowers the barrier for entry.[25] In a study on best practices in recruiting hidden populations via social media for qualitative research, Sikkens et al[26] suggest that researchers avoid polarizing terms in their initial call for study participants. After participants have contacted the researcher about the study, the researcher can fully explain the purpose of the study and contextualize any potentially polarizing language. This is the way that Sikkens et al[27] were able to recruit and study teenagers with radical and extremist political views with full participant consent. Utilizing more neutral terms and phrasing such as passive participation, reading without commenting, or silent observation, can entice prospective participants. Once prospective participants have answered the call, this is when the full context of the study can be disclosed and the researcher can, through informed consent, share that the research involves studying lurkers or lurking. This is an opportunity for the researcher to clarify any questions by the prospective participant and to ensure that they understand that they are consenting to participate in a study about lurking.

Since lurking is a context-specific practice, there will be some participants who are comfortable with public engagement on the platform where others will strongly resist leaving a visible trace of their engagement. When making the decision to lurk, people are concerned about data collection from the platform, but also from mediated lurking by other members of the group.[28] Therefore, providing an off-platform method for collecting the responses of prospective participants is likely to generate more responses. In other words, inviting participants to comment or engage in direct messaging on the platform will limit the number of people willing to participate in a study about lurking. Instead, including an email address, a Google Form, a Qualtrics link, or anything that will take the prospective participant to a more private location to signal their interest will yield a more robust response.

The Association for Internet Researchers (AoIR) offers very specific guidelines for consent. Three iterations of the AoIR Guideline for Ethical Consent exist. The section on Consent from the 2012 version should be considered in light of lurkers as participants.

> How are we recognizing the autonomy of others and acknowledging that they are of equal worth to ourselves and should be treated so?

- Will informed consent be required from participants?
- If so, what procedures to obtain consent will be followed? (E.g., print or digital signatures, virtual consent tokens, click boxes or waiver of documented consent.)
- Will consent be obtained just from individuals or from communities and online system administrators?
- In situations whereby consent is desired but written informed consent is impossible (or in regulatory criteria, impracticable) or potentially harmful, will procedures or requirements be modified?

- What harm might result from asking for consent, or through the process of asking for consent?
- What ethical concerns might arise if informed consent is not obtained?
- If an ethics board deems no consent is required, will the researcher still seek subjects'/participants' consent in a non-regulatory manner?
- If informed consent is warranted, how will the researcher ensure that participants are truly informed?[29]

Implications of not including lurkers

Lack of diverse participants

As discussed in Chapter 5, to be a lurker and to choose to withhold engagement is a privilege. There is also an overreliance on university student populations when conducting studies related to lurking. 'Findings derived from studies with US participants, often undergraduate students, are hardly a perfect representation of the diverse audiences in Europe, Latin America and Africa, and should be taken with caution.'[30] We are missing adult demographics: the group of people who have the most agency and currency with which to socially act upon what they have read.

Overreliance on platform perceptions

It is important to be wary of exclusively relying on the tools provided by platforms to collect data because they often obscure information about lurking. Facebook's CrowdTangle is an example of a tool that has iterated from an independent tool to a platform sponsored tool. In 2011 CrowdTangle launched as a civic technology that would allow individuals to organize activism on Facebook and by 2013 it had secured funding from the Knight Foundation to scale.[31] In its early years it was a centralized place where activists could link together Facebook pages, events, and groups. This was particularly helpful during the Occupy Wall Street Movement where CrowdTangle developed the Occupy Network, which connected over 1,669,000 people across 486 Occupy groups.[32] By aggregating this data, Occupy Network was a vital resource for activists seeking to join or expand the movement, journalists writing about the movement, and researchers studying it. Perhaps the most valuable part of CrowdTangle, at this time, was its ability to organize information and determine the most popular posts across groups and to view which Facebook friends were interacting. This made it easy to invite Facebook friends to join other local groups or share information about events. It was also a way to promote the cause to Facebook friends who were not actively posting, but who were affiliated with at least one of the groups, events, or pages.

In 2016, CrowdTangle was acquired by Facebook and the evolution of the tool was shaped to fit Facebook's mission and agenda. Initially

CrowdTangle retained operational autonomy within Facebook. The tool offered unparalleled access to trending topics on public facing accounts and communities across Facebook, Instagram, and Twitter. By 2019, Facebook created a more official relationship between CrowdTangle and academic researchers with its CrowdTangle for academics and researchers community. This initiative aimed to 'provide more transparency into how information is being spread on social media'.[33] Early partnerships were developed with University of California, Berkeley, Duke University, and the University of Münster for researchers studying misinformation and election integrity. Journalist Kevin Roose developed, in his words, 'a kludgey workaround' within CrowdTangle to rank Facebook posts that contain a link to a non-Facebook site.[34] He began a Twitter account called @FacebookTop10 to publish a daily listing of the top ten most-engaged links on US Facebook pages as measured by comments, reactions, and shares aggregated through CrowdTangle.[35] This account garnered over 35,000 followers by 2021 and has over 44,000 in 2022. Through promoting the most engaged links on Facebook, it became clear that conservative and President Trump aligned commentators like Ben Shapiro and news organizations like Fox News and Breitbart were consistently trending.[36] Then, in 2021, according to reporting by Roose for the *New York Times*, CrowdTangle staffing was reorganized under the integrity team in an attempt to 'rid the [Facebook] platform of misinformation and hate speech'.[37] This shift to management by the integrity team was a response to the increasing news coverage of Facebook as a 'right wing echo chamber',[38] which Facebook executives found troubling to the platform's brand.[39]

In late 2020 I was granted access to CrowdTangle as a researcher working on digital literacies. I was originally excited to join what was, at that time, a small group of researchers; however, it proved to be a mediocre tool for gathering data on lurking. CrowdTangle is a powerful tool for popularity rankings based on engagement, which measures public-facing metrics like comments, reactions, and shares. Data on reach, which measures the number of views and would be of great value in studying lurking as a reading practice, was not yet available. That same year Facebook CEO Mark Zuckerberg said in an interview with Axios on HBO, 'It's true that partisan content often has kind of a higher percent of people ... engaging with it, commenting on it, liking it. But I think it's important to differentiate that from, broadly, what people are seeing and reading and learning about on our service.' Zuckerberg's statements on the difference between engagement and reading made me hopeful that CrowdTangle would grow to offer more robust research opportunities, particularly in the area of reach. What I did not anticipate was that the way Facebook would ultimately seek to share data on reach was through its own independent research disseminated through blog posts and datasets.[40] It is technologically possible to offer researchers the ability to aggregate reach data on CrowdTangle in the same ways that it provides access to engagement data. Instead, Facebook decided to share its data by self-publishing its own independent research, which cannot be easily verified or peer-reviewed. This, coupled with the platform's reluctance to share any information on private or secret groups and pages, limits CrowdTangle's ability to collect data on lurking. During this time reports surfaced that the tool was becoming unreliable and producing erratic results from what appeared to be a lack of maintenance.[41] Not surprisingly, Meta, Facebook's now parent organization, has announced plans to dismantle the tool entirely.[42]

Even before the planned erosion of CrowdTangle began, in its heyday, CrowdTangle lacked the ability to offer context and nuance surrounding the shares. It was difficult to determine which links were being shared because one was affirming the content or the links were shared by someone offering divergent thought and analysis. Filtering for fact-checked or labelled posts was not an option. Under the management of the pre-Facebook-integrity-unit-CrowdTangle this information might have been easier to gather.[43] It is important to remember that despite the many limitations of CrowdTangle and its impending doom, CrowdTangle was the most robust public research tool available from a social media platform. X, TikTok, and YouTube do not even offer a sliver of what was possible on CrowdTangle.

When we rely on the tools built and/or maintained by platforms, our research serves at the whim of the platform. The dissolution of CrowdTangle is not the first time an extremely valuable search tool has vanished. Graph Search on Facebook was a tool that made it possible to search by photos, people, places, and interests.[44] The tool afforded the opportunity to create wildly specific searches of the voluminous information shared by Facebook account holders that when satirically queried by British YouTuber Tom Scott, generated intrusive results. A list of married people who like prostitutes among his Facebook network is but one example.[45] But Graph Search also offered researchers and activists the ability 'to locate and verify eyewitness footage on the platform, and document human rights abuses'.[46] This was in part because the open source intelligence community built third-party tools, like VanEss and StalkScan, that could search with even greater precision. When Graph Search was eliminated, the tools built by the open source intelligence community also imploded. It is a rather audacious proposition, but the tool that replaces CrowdTangle should be one purposefully designed by researchers and activists to allow access to both engagement and reach metrics. Developing a collaborative and autonomously managed tool to disrupt the proprietary hold on engagement, hover, and micro-metrics would be vital to furthering research on lurking.

Potentially flawed findings

Given the significant research on the behavioural normalcy of lurking, we can no longer exclude passive participation from our studies. Avoiding lurkers or noting the difficulty of recruiting them in a study can potentially lead to flawed findings. This is particularly important for the vast number of internet researchers engaged in studies of physical and mental health.

Conclusion: Participatory. And Valuable?

Although the introduction to this book begins in jest with the recollection of my mother-in-law calling me a lurker, I did not embark on this project with the goal of glorifying or lionizing lurking. In the initial phases of my research when I first came across boyd's question, 'Can someone be a valuable and participatory lurker?',[1] I used this question as an entry point to begin to better understand the positionality of the lurker among the members of the networked audience. By doing so, it soon became clear that there was indeed significant literature to demonstrate lurking as a participatory act and to disrupt the binary distinction of lurkers and contributors. As time progressed I focused less on lurkers as a discrete class of people and instead shifted towards lurker as a descriptor for digital literacies and literacy practices. In the early stages of drafting this book I had originally titled the Conclusion, 'Participatory and Valuable'. The more I spoke with others, though, whether it be participants for a study, colleagues, or even family and friends, there was a persistent patina around the idea that lurking could be valuable. This is in part because of the historicization of the term lurking, as outlined in Chapter 1, and its shifts in meaning over time to become connotative of predatory behaviour. But this resistance to classifying lurking as valuable is also linked to the ways in which passive participation is associated with bystanding within an increasingly toxic social media hellscape.[2] Therefore, as this book works its way towards conclusion, I wish to end on an interrogative, rather than a full stop: Participatory. And Valuable?

Lurkers *can* be valuable

Connotatively valuable can imply a moral or ethical good and lurking can be a benevolent or benign action as explored in Chapters 3 and 4 in regard to receptive reading, participatory restraint, sensemaking, protective curation, and reflexive entertainment. My choice of verbiage is intentional: the verb 'can' denotes the possibility, but not the requirement. Moral or ethical goodness is but one definition of value. When I first started my research, I focused on the verb 'is' rather than on the verb 'can' because the definition of valuable is not limited to moral or ethical goodness. Valuable is also synonymous with importance and that importance can be financially lucrative or politically powerful. In regard to this second definition of valuable,[3] financial and political value does not have to be in the best interest of humanity. Profit and power are valuable effects of lurking. Where a great number of the examples in this book explore lurker literacies and literacy practices that could connotatively be considered valuable in an ethical or humane sense, lurking can also be a valuable literacy practice for those with immoral or dangerous motives. As alluded to in the Introduction, the 6 January 2021 US Capitol autogolpe organized on the now castrated social media platform Parler is but one example of the way that the incendiary words and images one might read can lead to collective violent offline action.[4] The degree to which one is lurking for either benevolent or malevolent motives is not fixed, because as discussed in Chapter 2, lurking, like reading, is socially situated. Lurking produces profit and power for platforms, communities, businesses, and society.

Platforms

Lurkers are a financially valuable asset to the platforms that host them. Social media conglomerates like Meta primarily generate revenue through targeted advertisements. The ability of Facebook, for example, to command high advertising fees is because it can sell unparalleled exposure with a global audience of over 2.1 billion user accounts.[5] In *The Platform Society*, scholars Jose van Dijck, Thomas Poell, and Martijn De Waal explain that platforms are 'fueled by data' through a three-pronged process of datafication, commodification, and selection. As Nick Srnicek explains in his book, *Platform Capitalism*, platforms pursue all methods possible to collect and analyse the largest amount of data possible because the network effects a large and a diverse sample is what helps maintain a competitive economic advantage.[6] Therefore, registered membership numbers matter. Facebook has been involved in several lawsuits for allegedly inflating its account numbers on multiple occasions.[7] The financial advantage of being able to declare user dominance is in part why Facebook maintains the user accounts of an estimated 10–30 million deceased people[8] and a quarter of the platform is projected to one day be composed of the dead.[9] If the dead, who cannot click, hover, or scroll, can provide value, imagine what a living lurker provides? Beyond classification as an active user, which is defined by industry reports as having a pulse and not being attached to a memorial account, the micro-movements, views, plays, click-through links, and hovers one engages in while on the platform can all be monetized.[10] This monetization is in the form of data sold to advertisers on trending content and the type of content that leads to actionable, traceable engagement.

Further proof of the value lurkers provide to platforms includes the way platforms capitalize on lurking as participation. If you ever look at someone's public Instagram or Twitter (prior to the transformation to X) while not logged into the platform you are allowed to freely view a few posts. After a few quick scrolls, you are met with a pop-up window indicating that if you would like to see more, you must log in. At first glance this gesture might look like a way to protect the privacy of the account holder. However, this is true for even account holders who have marked their account as public. One might be an entrepreneur or a content creator seeking the benefits of having new audiences find their words and work. This kind of exposure is valuable to the entrepreneur or a content creator regardless of whether that audience logs into the platform or not. Platforms seeking to capitalize on the value that lurking provides force the audience member to make a decision about whether or not to login. If the reader logs in, they have the opportunity to become a member of the networked audience and engage along the efferent–aesthetic continuum of new literacies as discussed in Chapter 2. If upon logging in they then choose to continue lurking, the platform will find this permissible because it contributes to the extraction of data the platform can sell to potential advertisers. The person engaged in lurking will, of course, be nudged to engage in publicity metrics both on and off platform. On-platform nudges include notifications and algorithmically curated feeds based on hovering and reading patterns. Despite these nudges to publicly participate, it is not necessary to do so if you wish to continue reading. The data collected from on-platform reading is valuable enough. When a Twitter account holder has not logged in in a while, they will receive off-platform nudges to their email. I have a few secondary and tertiary Twitter accounts that I do not frequently use and, prior to the transformation to X, I received daily emails with subject lines that read 'Check out the notifications you have', 'Did you see that great tweet', 'Penny for your thoughts', and in a Kollock and Smith throwback,[11] 'Don't be selfish'. Twitter strategically used this rhetorical series of phrases in the subject lines to prompt the kind of platform-controlled engagement that will broker a transaction of data extraction to maximize profitability.

At the time of this writing, Twitter has recently been acquired by billionaire business magnate Elon Musk whose executive changes to the platform have yet to be fully implemented. As Twitter attempts to rebrand as X, the platform has made several strategic decisions to capitalize on the financial value that lurkers provide. In the transition to X, public account access is no longer available, for even a modicum of posts, unless you are an account holder logged in to the platform. The most notable change that has occurred from Musk's acquisition of Twitter is the decision to charge users for blue check verification status. Where in the past such verification was determined by professional merit, one had to be deemed 'authentic', 'notable', and 'active' in government, media, business, or entertainment to warrant verification that the name associated with the account is the same as the person composing the tweets. In 2022 an option became available to purchase a blue check through Twitter Blue subscriptions, now called X Premium. Those who can afford to and choose to purchase the blue check for their account will hold the blue check designation for the duration of their subscription. Aside from the perceived prestige of being blue-check verified, accounts with X Premium receive priority in replies, mentions, and searches. Notably, X Premium accounts also have access to Reader Mode, described by the company as 'a more beautiful reading experience, without the noise'.[12] These account holders also have the option to post longer videos and receive fewer targeted advertisements. The array of features available to X Premium customers enhances the reading experiences in ways that make lurking an easier and more enjoyable experience for those who can afford verification.

In 2021, blue-check verification was initially only available in the United States, Canada, Australia, New Zealand, and the United Kingdom for those utilizing a mobile iOS. These changes shifted who among the networked audience could primarily post with influence, and who was restricted to primarily reading or lurking. The thoughts and ideas of the Anglophone West had the compulsory attention of account holders in Latin America, the Middle East, Asia, and continental Europe. Lurking was not a choice; it was a prescribed position.

Although X Premium has recently begun to offer worldwide service, its price in August 2023 has jumped from US$8 per month for web browser access and US$11 per month for iOS and Android users to up to US$16 per month, depending on the geographic location and tier of the subscriber.[13] This is a prohibitive price point for academics, many of whom are underemployed. Moreover, the rollout to the global Twitter Blue service also came with further restrictions on reading.[14] Without a premium subscription, an X account holder in 2023 can only read 600 posts per day; a new or recently subscribed X account holder can only read 300. In August 2023 that number was recently lifted to 1,000 posts for current account holders. A limit of any kind, however, creates a geography of exclusion to lurking. Attempting to read more than the daily allotted posts will result in a locked account. Although Musk asserts that the restrictions are temporary, no end date has yet to be announced.

Another downstream effect of this subscription-based X Premium is the shift towards vacuous verification. In the early days of the Musk-led takeover of the platform, downsizing efforts have gutted the departments responsible for content regulation on Twitter. This, coupled with the pay-to-play participation of Twitter Blue, means that the platform is poised to receive an onslaught of fake and parody accounts. For these reasons, academics on Twitter threatened for the months leading up to Musk's official takeover that they would leave the platform in search of quiet communities. Mastodon, at the moment, is the platform of choice. Mastodon's small size and scale is part of the allure. With Twitter blue-check accounts positioned to dominate the content stream, the unchecked Twitter account holders are concerned that the content they read will be overwhelmed by posts in the 8Chan or PornHub genre. Conversely, some of the early migrants to Mastodon have been stifled by the way that its decentralized federation of instances creates a siloed effect for readers. Unlike Twitter/X, where one can follow threads from physicists, poets, philosophers, and Kim Kardashian, in one casual scroll, on Mastodon one account can only belong to one instance. For example, someone cannot belong to both mastodon.social and mastodon. design, although one can follow accounts on any instance. This makes for a more conscious and concerted curatorial effort on the part of the Mastodon account holder. It is yet to be determined which platform, X, Mastodon, or some other yet-to-be-known platform, will emerge victorious, but the winner will be the one that makes lurking an easy and pleasurable experience.

Communities

Lurking can be a leisurely pursuit that builds an offline community. With the market for network television being squeezed out by cable options that are becoming more and more expensive to access, people look to streaming apps to achieve gratifications similar to those once sought from broadcast media. The early days of radio and television were a time when people would meet their family, friends, and neighbours to gather together around the device. The exorbitant cost of a new radio or television meant that there were few who could afford one, and those who could probably only had one device in their home. Narrative accounts of the early days of radio and television are nostalgic about the community connections and the shared experience of listening and viewing together. Social media streaming on networked applications like Twitch are creating a similarly valuable experience where offline communities are developing for watching and being together.

On Twitch, professional gamers, for example, live-stream their games. Gamer communities are built in response to these streams. This offline community is not necessarily built around a transactional monetary exchange (although I will discuss these kinds of fiscal transactions in the next section). They are a place where gaming fans, including those with lower levels of expertise, come together to watch and learn. Community members make offline plans to play the games together while watching the stream and listening to the streamer discuss their strategy. The command !lurk is utilized by community members who wish to indicate that they will be lurking and not participating in comments or likes. The intrinsic value these lurker community members experience is at odds with the profit value the Twitch platform prioritizes.

There has been significant controversy on Twitch surrounding the role of lurk views and whether or not the platform will allow lurk views to count towards the required number of views for a streaming content creator to level up to affiliate status. On Twitch, anyone can create content, but the creator cannot profit from their channel until they achieve affiliate status or the 'coveted' rank of Twitch Partner.[15] In order to progress to either status, a content creator must meet targeted benchmarks in followers, streaming hours per day, and viewer count per stream. As a platform, Twitch's temporary decision to suspend lurk views in the targeted benchmark count caused uproar among content producers.[16] It was also offensive to those who enjoy these communities to be disregarded as irrelevant by the platform. When platforms issue guidelines around who counts as a real fan, and deny the legitimate participation of lurkers, it misrepresents what is happening in these communities. The vociferous outpouring of support by both content producers and the fans within and beyond the lurker communities forced the Twitch platform to rethink its decision.

Businesses

The shift to a promotion economy centres the necessity of the lurker. With more and more people looking to supplement their income through gig and contingent digital pursuits, sustainable revenue relies on a strong base of lurkers. Streamers on Twitch are not the only ones who rely on what the Twitch platform calls 'lurk views' as an important part of their personal revenue stream. People who lurk on Twitch help to boost the content producer's view count and move them towards affiliate status. Once a content producer achieves affiliate status, their revenue significantly increases.

Beyond viewing, the !lurk command can be utilized by community members who want to show their support, but who cannot or choose not to participate in direct fiscal engagement. Since much of the direct engagement on Twitch is linked to monetary compensation in the form of cash donations, Twitch bits (Twitch's in-house currency), and subscriptions, lurk communities offer a way to gather beyond transactional exchange. Content creators on Twitch financially depend on and are gratified by the support of lurkers. This is evident in the trove of online resources available for content creators who want to 'lure the lurkers'.[17]

Those seeking to build large followings on subscription-based platforms like Substack depend on lurkers to build their community. The pricing structure on Substack relies on the total number of followers, regardless of participatory activity. For example, if you have a substantial following of 20,000 paid Substack subscribers and 15,000 of them are lurkers who subscribe and read your work but never leave comments – you're still getting paid. Lurkers are a sizable portion of your income that are actively sought by content creators.

An organizational study of the US Major League Baseball (MLB) found that lurkers on fan forums attend more games and buy more merchandise then 'active' participants who frequently comment.[18] As established in Chapter 5, lurking is a privileged position and there is a correlation between higher income and higher degrees of lurking. Participation in real-world MLB games and events is extraordinarily expensive. Individual general admission tickets for the Arizona Diamondbacks MLB game, the least expensive in the league, is US$21.38 per person.[19] This is in contrast with the Chicago Cubs, where the highest priced general admission tickets in the league clock in at US$57.82 per person.[20] When the cost of parking and refreshments is included in the equation, the cost rises to US$46.13 and US$110.17, respectively, per person.[21] The escalated cost of attendance and consumption means that access is reserved for those with the highest amount of disposable income.

Autoethnographic reflections on the value of lurking

These days it is unfashionable to be publicly active on Facebook. Nearly ten years after I removed myself from active Facebook commenting, the geriatric platform reported to its investors in February of 2022 that for the first time its daily active users dropped by more than 500,000 people and that its monthly active users had plateaued.[22] Where Facebook has not released information on how many people have deleted their Facebook accounts, a survey in 2018 conducted by the Pew Research Center in response to the Cambridge Analytica scandal revealed that over a quarter of all surveyed Facebook users had deleted the app from their phone.[23] As an early abandoner, who never downloaded the app and has yet to permanently delete my account, I have spent ten years honing my lurker literacies. In the Introduction I questioned whether or not my reasons for lurking were justifiable. Another way to consider this question is to reflect on whether or not participating in lurker literacies has been a valuable personal experience.

Since their birth, I have taken thousands of digital photos of my children. Only two photographs, announcing their respective births, have been shared (by me) on Facebook. The domestic maintenance of sharing photographs, captioning, and engaging with commenters requires a time commitment beyond what I can or wish to spend on the platform. For my in-laws who live nearly 300 miles away and are always eager to keep tabs on what the children are doing, I instead created a Google Photo album and an iPhone home screen shortcut to the album for easy access. In the same way that my own grandparents nearly 40 years ago would carry my school photograph in a plastic protector in their wallet, always easily accessible to share with a neighbour or the postal worker, my in-laws can always reach for their phone and share a picture face-to-face with a friend. Unlike the Facebook 'friend' with whom you may have a tenuous relationship, the effort required to reach into your pocket, unlock your phone, tap, swipe, and scroll to locate the photo, creates a more selective opportunity for sharing photos.

In addition to my work as a scholar of literacy, media, and technology I am also a poet. Over the past decade I have explored my relationship to technology through this medium and in a version of a poem published in *The Paterson Literary Review* in 2014, I wrote about the impact posting (and not posting) would have on the children I imagined I might one day have.

The 'Why I hate Facebook' poem

A friend on the West Coast demands to know why I haven't posted photos of my new house on Facebook because how else is she going to see it? I gently remind her that she could visit. Annoyed, she doesn't speak to me for six months.

I've only had one real fight with my best friend of twenty years and it was over the one time I posted several words in support of Planned Parenthood. I never posted a political opinion, of any stripe, ever again.

My cousin's fiancée breaks up with him and he posts a series of YouTube videos where he plays a melancholy piano and sobs through *Ain't No Mountain High Enough*. His father posts underneath, *Stop being a pussy. Nobody wants to watch this.*

A middle school friend who used to keep a pet bat in a cage, and dated a guy who wore black eyeliner and half a garden hose as a belt, types daily #jesuslovesyou affirmations underneath photos of her blond-haired family in Vineyard Vines.

My dead friend Misty has had more status updates then me in the past year and she populates my feed every #tbt.

I have a short list of ex-boyfriends with pending friend requests, but I have no idea how my privacy settings really work, so I am afraid to accept them. Their avatars sit in limbo for years awaiting my reply. When I saw one of them face-to-face at a reunion, he said that he thought it was a passive aggressive way of getting back at him for a call he never returned. I simply said, *Yes.*

Students I taught when they were eleven are now eighteen and
twenty and post selfies in scantily clad attire, sometimes drunk,
sometimes high, and I don't know if they don't remember I'm
on their list of friends or if they simply don't care.

I wonder about my friends who document their children's
lives from sonogram to soccer star. Will their children be
embarrassed or angry in their adulthood?

Will mine think I don't love them because I haven't tagged their
image for the world to see?

The interrogative introduced at the poem's conclusion, for me, is a constant
question. It has been valuable to be present and not feel the need to curate
our family life for an audience. I do curate photos to include in our shared
family album, but I have turned off comments and push notifications.
The photos are broadcasted, but not networked. To have a conversation
about the events photographed and collected in the album requires a text,
a phone call, or a visit to decipher the context for the images or to share a
response. Where I use LinkedIn and X to professionally connect with my
colleagues, and rely on my neighbourhood Facebook groups to subscribe
to local information, I have made a wholehearted decision to live most of
my social existence offline.

Ultimately it is the communities that people form, their purpose and their
values that will impact the degree to which lurking is helpful or not. As
new technologies emerge, their ability to provide pathways for connection,
amplification, and scale will shift the magnitude of a lurker's impact. The
many stigmas surrounding lurking that this book addresses is what drew
me to conduct further independent research into connotatively valuable
practices. This book is an attempt at adding these stories to the narrative
of what it means to lurk. It is not an argument to remove the word from
our lexicon. Rather I am interested in shifting towards the use of the word
lurker as an adjective to describe a certain way of reading. I am looking to
contextualize the term rather than dismiss it.

Notes

Introduction

[1] The now defunct online *Jargon Dictionary* contains one of the earliest uses of the word delurk, stating that '[w]hen a lurker speaks up for the first time, this is called "delurking"'. A reference to this post on delurking can be found in R.B. Nonnecke (2000) *Lurking in Email Based Distribution Lists*. [Dissertation] Available at: https://citeseerx.ist.psu.edu/document?repid=rep1&type=pdf&doi=55fb98dc5295dd7c6b3e95f5202fe7c7b6f2809e [Accessed 7 December 2022]. Since that time, delurking has become a standardized term within scholarship on lurking to describe the transition from lurker to participant, often within a binary view of participation.

[2] Wishing someone a happy birthday on social media, Facebook in particular, has been the site of interdisciplinary scholarship on social norms, etiquette, and expectations. Among the many studies of the decision whether or not to wish someone a happy birthday, see E. Bryant and J. Marmo (2009) Relational maintenance strategies on Facebook, *Kentucky Journal of Communication*, [online] 28(2), pp 129–150. Available at: https://digitalcommons.trinity.edu/cgi/viewcontent.cgi?article=1005&context=hct_faculty [Accessed 7 December 2022] for a nuanced discussion of the choices one makes in whether to post or withhold from posting. Although Bryant and Marmo do not use the term lurk, their lens of relational maintenance is helpful in destigmatizing and humanizing the complex decision-making calculus one considers before they decide whether or not to lurk.

[3] M. Sullivan (2014) Zuckerberg reiterates: You have to use your real name on Facebook, *VentureBeat* [online]. Available at: https://venturebeat.com/social/zuckerberg-reiterates-you-have-to-use-your-real-name-on-facebook/ [Accessed 7 December 2022].

[4] Context collapse was first described in J. Meyrowitz (1985) *No Sense of Place: The Impact of Electronic Media on Social Behavior*, New York: Oxford University Press. Meyrowitz relied on foundational analysis by Erving Goffman to explore how emerging broadcast technologies like radio and television create a flattened and narrow experience for the audience. Goffman has previously used the term 'audience segregation' to describe how one, as a social actor, performs differently depending upon the audience. Context collapse was later applied to digital spaces in d. boyd (2001) *Faceted Id/entity: Managing Representation in a Digital World*. [Doctoral dissertation], Brown University. Available at: http://www.danah.org/papers/Thesis.FacetedIdentity.pdf [Accessed 5 November 2023].

[5] For a glimpse at the picquote, see PictureQuotes.com (nd) You can't be neutral on a moving train [online]. Available at: http://www.picturequotes.com/you-cant-be-neutral-on-a-moving-train-quote-442732 [Accessed 7 December 2022]. The original source for Howard Zinn's quotation comes from his memoir, of the same name: H. Zinn (2002) *You Can't Be Neutral on a Moving Train: A Personal History*, Boston: Beacon Press.

6   For some of the structural reasons, see A. Romano (2018) How Facebook made it impossible to delete Facebook, *Vox* [online]. Available at: https://www.vox.com/cult ure/2018/3/22/17146776/delete-facebook-how-to-quit-difficult [Accessed 5 November 2023]. For information on the struggles and the benefits, if successfully quitting Facebook, see H. Allcott, L. Braghieri, S. Eichmeyer, and M. Gentzkow (2020) The welfare effects of social media, *American Economic Review*, 110(3), pp 629–676. M. Tromholt (2016) The Facebook experiment: Quitting Facebook leads to higher levels of well-being, *Cyberpsychology, Behavior, and Social Networking*, 19(11), pp 661–666.

7   This was in the early days before it was fashionable to leave Facebook in a dramatic flourish over privacy concerns. See coverage of the #DeleteFacebook movement: A. Perrin (2018) Americans are changing their relationship with Facebook, *Pew Research Center* [online]. Available at: https://www.pewresearch.org/fact-tank/2018/09/05/americans-are-chang ing-their-relationship-with-facebook/ [Accessed 5 November 2023]. Also see Facebook co-founder and former employee Chris Hughes' op-ed for the *New York Times*: C. Hughes (2019) It's time to break up Facebook, *The New York Times* [online] 9 May. Available at: https:// www.nytimes.com/2019/05/09/opinion/sunday/chris-hughes-facebook-zuckerberg.html [Accessed 9 May 2019].

8   N. Sun, P.P.L. Rau, and L. Ma (2014) Understanding lurkers in online communities: A literature review, *Computers in Human Behavior*, 38, pp 100–117; S. Honeychurch, A. Bozkurt, L. Singh, and A. Koutropoulos (2017) Learners on the periphery: Lurkers as invisible learners, *European Journal of Open, Distance and E-Learning*, 21(1), pp 192–211; and N. Edelmann, R. Krimmer, and P. Parycek (2017) How online lurking contributes value to e-participation: A conceptual approach to evaluating the role of lurkers in e-participation, *Fourth International Conference on eDemocracy & eGovernment (ICEDEG) IEEE*, Quito, Ecuador, pp 86–93.

9   S. Fox and L. Rainie (2014) Part 1: How the internet has woven itself into American life, *Pew Research Center* [online]. Available at: https://www.pewresearch.org/internet/ 2014/02/27/part-1-how-the-internet-has-woven-itself-into-american-life/ [Accessed 5 November 2023].

10 R. Lindsey (1983) Computer as letterbox, singles bar and seminar, *The New York Times*, 2 December. Available at: https://www.nytimes.com/1983/12/02/us/computer-as-letter box-singles-bar-and-seminar.html [Accessed 5 November 2023].

11 J. Katz (1998) Luring the lurkers, *Slashdot*. Available at: http://slashdot.org/features/98/ 12/28/1745252.shtml [Accessed 5 November 2023].

12 B. Nonnecke and J. Preece (2001) Why lurkers lurk, in paper presented at the Americas conference on information systems conference, Boston. Nonnecke, J. Preece, and D. Andrews (2004) What lurkers and posters think of each other, *Proceedings of the 37th Hawaii International Conference on System Science*. Available at: http://www.cis.uoguelph.ca/ ~nonnecke/research/whylurk.pdf [Accessed 5 November 2023]. B. Nonnecke, J. Preece, D. Andrews, and B. Voutour (2004) Online lurkers tell why they lurk, in paper presented at the 10th Americas conference on information systems, New York. Available at: http:// www.cis.uoguelph.ca/~nonnecke/research/OnlineLurkersTellWhy.pdf [Accessed 5 November 2023].

13 There will be further discussion of Rosenblatt's theory of efferent and aesthetic reading experience in Chapter 3. L.M. Rosenblatt (1994) *The Reader, the Text, the Poem: The Transactional Theory of the Literary Work*, Carbondale: Southern Illinois University Press.

14 P. Kollock and M. Smith (1996) Managing the virtual commons: Cooperation and conflict in computer communities, in S.C. Herring (ed) *Computer Mediated Communication: Linguistic, Social, and Cross-Cultural Perspectives*, Amsterdam: John Benjamins, pp 109–128.

15 H. Jenkins, M. Itō, and d. boyd (2016) *Participatory Culture in a Networked Era: A Conversation on Youth, Learning, Commerce, and Politics*, Cambridge: Polity, p 112.

16 Jenkins does later go on to explore the potential value of lurking in further depth in H. Jenkins, S. Ford, and J. Green (2013) *Spreadable Media: Creating Value and Meaning in a Networked Culture*, New York: New York University Press.

17 J. Preece, B. Nonnecke, and D. Andrews (2004) The top five reasons for lurking: Improving community experiences for everyone, *Computers in Human Behavior*, 20, pp 201–223.

18 D. Barton and M. Hamilton (2000) Literacy practices, in D. Barton, M. Hamilton, and R. Ivanic (eds) *Situated Literacies: Reading and Writing in Context*, London: Routledge, pp 7–15.

19 H.J. Graff (1988) The legacies of literacy, in E. Kintgen, B. Kroll, and M. Rose (eds) *Perspectives of Literacy*, Carbondale: Southern Illinois University Press, pp 137–172.

20 Chapter 5 will discuss these ideas in greater depth utilizing the research by W. James Potter. See W.J. Potter (2022) Analysis of definitions of media literacy, *Journal of Media Literacy Education*, 14(2), pp 27–43; and W.J. Potter (2010) The state of media literacy, *Journal of Broadcasting & Electronic Media*, 54(4), pp 675–696.

21 d. boyd (2018) What hath we wrought? *danah boyd SXSW EDU Keynote* [online]. Available at: https://www.youtube.com/watch?time_continue=16&v=0I7FVyQCjNg [Accessed 13 January 2023].

22 This is a starting point for some of the robust scholarship on the effect of media literacy on shaping election results: H. Jenkins, M. Itō, and d. boyd (2016) *Participatory Culture in a Networked Era: A Conversation on Youth, Learning, Commerce, and Politics*, Cambridge: Polity; W. Phillips and R.M. Milner (2017) *The Ambivalent Internet: Mischief, Oddity, and Antagonism Online*, Cambridge, MA: Polity; W. Phillips and R.M. Milner (2021) *You Are Here: A Field Guide for Navigating Polluted Information*, Cambridge, MA: MIT Press.

23 K. Swisher (2021) If you were on Parler, you saw the mob coming, *The New York Times* [online] 7 January. Available at: https://www.nytimes.com/2021/01/07/opinion/sway-kara-swisher-john-matze.html [Accessed 7 December 2022]. The Parler app has since met with its own uncertain future when it was implicated as an autogolpe organizing tool in the attacks on the US Capitol. The app was initially removed from Apple's App store and the Google Play store. Amazon has also removed web hosting privileges for Parler's web-based application, a decision upheld by the U.S. District Court in Western Washington state, see E. Culliford and J. Stempel (2021) Parler loses bid to require Amazon to restore service, *Reuters* [online] 21 January. Available at: https://www.reuters.com/article/us-amazon-com-parler-idUSKBN29Q2T3 [Accessed 19 January 2023]. At the time of this writing, Parler has recently been reinstated on Apple's App store, the Google Play store, and through web-based hosting with Amazon.

24 W. Phillips (2022) *The Oxygen of Amplification*. Report. Data & Society [online]. Available at: https://datasociety.net/library/oxygen-of-amplification/ [Accessed 5 November 2023].

Chapter 1

1 J.V. Smith (1991) *The Lurker*, New York: HarperCollins.

2 WorldCat (2023) Lurker: Search results. *WorldCat* [online]. Available at: https://www.worldcat.org/search?q=ti%3ALurker&itemType=book&itemSubType=book-printbook%2Cbook-digital%2Cbook-thsis [Accessed 19 January 2023].

3 C.N. Adichie (2009) The dangers of a single story. *TED*. Available at: https://www.ted.com/talks/chimamanda_ngozi_adichie_the_danger_of_a_single_story/transcript?language=en 2009 [Accessed 5 November 2023].

4 J.O. Halliwell-Phillipps and T. Wright (1845) *Reliquiæ Antiquæ: Scraps from Ancient Manuscripts, Illustrating Chiefly Early English Literature and the English Language*, Volume 1,

London: John Russell Smith. Available at: https://catalog.hathitrust.org/Record/001023 787 [Accessed 5 November 2023].

5   S. Heaney (trans) (1982) Names of the hare, in S. Heaney and T. Hughes (eds) *The Rattle Bag: An Anthology of Poetry*, London: Faber & Faber, pp 305–306.

6   J.M. Dean (ed) (2000) *Richard the Redeles and Mum the Sothseeger*, Kalamazoo: Medieval Institute Series.

7   Jeremiah 17:11, English Standard Version Bible (2001) ESV Online. Available at: https://esv.literalword.com/?h=11&q=Jeremiah+17 [Accessed 5 November 2023].

8   C. Cheesman (2008) Partridges: The history of a prohibition, *The Coat of Arms*, 4, pp 29–62.

9   Anonymous (1842) *An Exposure of the Various Impositions Daily Practised by Vagrants of Every Description*, Birmingham: J. Taylor.

10 Anonymous (1842) *An Exposure of the Various Impositions Daily Practised by Vagrants of Every Description*, Birmingham: J. Taylor.

11 *The Edinburgh Review* (1842) Mendicity its causes and statistics, *The Edinburgh Review*, CLII, pp 467–491.

12 H. Mahew (1851) *London Labour and the Poor*, Volume 1. Available at: https://www.gutenberg.org/files/55998/55998-h/55998-h.htm [Accessed 6 November 2023].

13 C. Dickens (1850) A walk in the workhouse, *Household Words*, 1(9), pp 204–207.

14 W. Gibson (2003) *Burning Chrome*, New York: Harper Voyager (reprint).

15 R. Lindsey (1983) Computer as letterbox, singles bar and seminar, *The New York Times*, 2 December. Available at: https://www.nytimes.com/1983/12/02/us/computer-as-letter box-singles-bar-and-seminar.html [Accessed 6 November 2023].

16 R. Lindsey (1983) Computer as letterbox, singles bar and seminar, *The New York Times*, 2 December. Available at: https://www.nytimes.com/1983/12/02/us/computer-as-letter box-singles-bar-and-seminar.html [Accessed 6 November 2023].

17 CompuServe (1984) Thanks to Compuserve's CB Simulator 'Digital Fox' accessed 'Data Hari' and proceeded to an 'Altared' state, *Byte* [Advert].

18 McGrath, C. (1996) The internet's, *The New York Times*, 8 December, pp SM80–SM84.

19 McGrath, C. (1996) The internet's, *The New York Times*, 8 December, pp SM80–SM84, at p SM83.

20 McGrath, C. (1996) The internet's, *The New York Times*, 8 December, pp SM83–SM84.

21 M.W. Ross (2005) Typing, doing, and being: Sexuality and the internet, *The Journal of Sex Research*, 42(4), pp 342–352, at p 348.

22 M.W. Ross (2005) Typing, doing, and being: Sexuality and the internet, *The Journal of Sex Research*, 42(4), pp 342–352, at p 348.

23 A.C. Seibt, M.W. Ross, A. Freeman, M. Krepcho, A. Hedrich, A. McAlister, et al (1995) Relationship between safe sex and acculturation into the gay subculture, *AIDS Care*, 7(Suppl. 1), pp S85–S88.

24 P. Kollock and M. Smith (1996) Cooperation and conflict in computer communities, in S.C. Herring (ed) *Computer-Mediated Communication: Linguistic, Social, and Cross-Cultural Perspectives*, Amsterdam: John Benjamins, pp 109–128, at p 109.

25 P. Kollock and M. Smith (1996) Cooperation and conflict in computer communities, in S.C. Herring (ed) *Computer-Mediated Communication: Linguistic, Social, and Cross-Cultural Perspectives*, Amsterdam: John Benjamins, pp 109–128, at p 109.

26 Unlike Kollock and Smith, Morris and Ogan use free riders as two separate words. See M. Morris and C. Ogan (1996) The internet as mass medium, *Journal of Communication*, 46(1), pp 39–50.

27   Discretionary database is a term first used by T. Connolly and B.K. Thorn (1991) Discretionary data bases: Theory, data, and implications, in J. Fulk and C. Steinfield (eds) *Organizations and Communication Technology*, Newbury Park: SAGE, pp 219–233.

28   B. Wellman and M. Gulia (1999) Netsurfers don't ride alone: Virtual communities as communities, in Barry Wellman (ed) *Networks in the Global Village*, New York: Routledge, pp 331–366.

29   R.B. Nonnecke (2000) *Lurking in Email Based Distribution Lists*. [Dissertation], p 95. Available at: https://citeseerx.ist.psu.edu/document?repid=rep1&type=pdf&doi= 55fb98dc5295dd7c6b3e95f5202fe7c7b6f2809e [Accessed 7 December 2022].

30   R.B. Nonnecke (2000) *Lurking in Email Based Distribution Lists*. [Dissertation] Available at: https://citeseerx.ist.psu.edu/document?repid=rep1&type=pdf&doi=55fb98dc5295d d7c6b3e95f5202fe7c7b6f2809e [Accessed 7 December 2022].

31   B. Nonnecke and J. Preece (2000) Lurker demographics, *Proceedings of the SIGCHI Conference on Human Factors in Computing Systems – CHI '00*. doi:10.1145/332040.332409.

32   R.B. Nonnecke (2000) *Lurking in Email Based Distribution Lists*. [Dissertation] Available at: https://citeseerx.ist.psu.edu/document?repid=rep1&type=pdf&doi=55fb98dc5295d d7c6b3e95f5202fe7c7b6f2809e [Accessed 7 December 2022].

33   B. Nonnecke and J. Preece (2001) Why lurkers lurk, in paper presented at the Americas conference on information systems conference, Boston http://www.cis.uoguelph.ca/ ~nonnecke/research/whylurk.pdf [Accessed 6 November 2023]; B. Nonnecke, J. Preece, D. Andrews, and B. Voutour (2004) Online lurkers tell why, in paper presented at the 10th Americas conference on information systems, New York Available at: http:// www.cis.uoguelph.ca/~nonnecke/research/OnlineLurkersTellWhy.pdf [Accessed 6 November 2023].

34   J. Preece, B. Nonnecke, and D. Andrews (2004) The top five reasons for lurking: improving community experiences for everyone, *Computers in Human Behavior*, 20(2), pp 201–223, at p 201.

35   See C. Fullwood, D. Chadwick, M. Keep, A. Attrill-Smith, T. Asbury, and G. Kirwan (2019) Lurking towards empowerment: Explaining propensity to engage with online health support groups and its association with positive outcomes, *Computers in Human Behavior*, 90, pp 131–140; C.F. van Uden-Kraan, C.H. Drossaert, E. Taal, B.R. Shaw, E.R. Seydel, and M.A. van de Laar (2008) Empowering processes and outcomes of participation in online support groups for patients with breast cancer, arthritis, or fibromyalgia, *Qualitative Health Research*, 18(3), pp 405–417.

36   S.A.A. Kasuma and D. Wray (2015) An informal Facebook Group for English language interaction: A study of Malaysian university students' perspectives, experiences and behaviours, paper presented at the 5th Annual International Conference on Education & e-learning (Eel 2015). Available at: https://www.researchgate.net/publication/ 301406262_An_informal_Facebook_group_for_English_language_interaction_A_study_ of_Malaysian_university_students'_perspectives_experiences_and_behaviours [Accessed 6 November 2023].

37   A. Webster (2016) Review: The 'trolls' embark on a high-haired rescue mission, *The New York Times* [online] 3 November. Available at: https://www.nytimes.com/2016/11/ 04/movies/trolls-review.html [Accessed 19 January 2023].

38   W. Phillips (2016) *This is Why We Can't Have Nice Things: Mapping the Relationship between Online Trolling and Mainstream Culture*, Cambridge, MA: MIT Press, p 24.

39   W. Phillips (2016) *This is Why We Can't Have Nice Things: Mapping the Relationship between Online Trolling and Mainstream Culture*, Cambridge, MA: MIT Press, p 25.

40 M. Wills (2017) Popcorn: From ancient snack to movie standby, *JSTOR Daily* [online]. Available at: https://daily.jstor.org/popcorn-from-ancient-snack-to-movie-standby/ [Accessed 6 November 2023].

41 M. Nänny and O. Fischer (2001) *The Motivated Sign: [A Selection of Papers Given at the Second International and Interdisciplinary Symposium]*, Amsterdam: Benjamins.

42 J. Lacan and J.-A. Miller (1988) *The Seminar of Jacques Lacan*, New York: Norton.

43 Lave and Wenger use the term legitimate peripheral participant to describe lurkers in J. Lave and E. Wenger (1991) *Situated Learning: Legitimate Peripheral Participation*, Cambridge: Cambridge University Press. Nonnecke suggests the term Non Public Participant in R.B. Nonnecke (2000) *Lurking in Email Based Distribution Lists*. [Dissertation]. Available at: https://citeseerx.ist.psu.edu/document?repid=rep1&type=pdf&doi=55fb98dc5295dd7c6b3e95f5202fe7c7b6f2809e [Accessed 7 December 2022].

Chapter 2

1 Versions of *Der Bücherwurm* can be found at https://en.dopl3r.com/memes/dank/me-at-3am-reading-all-388-comments-of-two-strangers-arguing-on-facebook-classical-art-memes-facebookcomclassicalartmemes/982491 and https://www.verbub.com/i/336088/me-at-3am-reading-all-388-comments-of-two-strangers-arguing-on [Accessed 6 November 2023].

2 C. Schleicher (1900) *Der Bücherwurm*. Oil on panel.

3 R. Barthes (1977) *Image-Music-Text: Roland Barthes*, translated by S. Heath, Glasgow: Collins.

4 L.M. Rosenblatt (1969) Towards a transactional theory of reading, *Journal of Reading Behavior*, 1(1), pp 31–49.

5 H. Jenkins, S. Ford, and J. Green (2018) *Spreadable Media: Creating Value and Meaning in a Networked Culture*, New York: New York University Press, p 155.

6 See Marwick's work on the networked audience: A. Marwick (2013) *Status Update: Celebrity, Publicity, and Branding in the Social Media Age*, New Haven: Yale University Press.

7 Jean Lave and Etiene Wenger describe online participation as either central or peripheral. J. Lave and E. Wenger (1991) *Situated Learning: Legitimate Peripheral Participation*, Cambridge: Cambridge University Press. Robert Blair Nonnecke describes participation as a fluctuating positionality between public and non-public. R.B. Nonnecke (2000) *Lurking in Email Based Distribution Lists*. [Dissertation] Available at: https://citeseerx.ist.psu.edu/document?repid=rep1&type=pdf&doi=55fb98dc5295dd7c6b3e95f5202fe7c7b6f2809e [Accessed 7 December 2022]. Jay Bolter describes online participation as a mixture of participants and consumers. J. Bolter (2001) *Writing Space: Computers, Hypertext, and the Remediation of Print*, Routledge: New York. Sanna Malinen gives an overview of the descriptors of active and passive online participation and their limits. S. Malinen (2015) Understanding user participation in online communities: A systematic literature review of empirical studies, *Computers in Human Behavior*, 46, pp 228–238. Although I am listing a few examples of places where these binary terms originate, they continue to persist in blog posts and influencer marketing on how to build digital audiences.

8 J. Luiten van Zanden, J. Baten, M. Mira d'Ercole, A. Rijpma, and M. Timmer (2014) *How Was Life? Global Well-being since 1820*, OECD iLibrary [online]. Available at: https://www.oecd-ilibrary.org/economics/how-was-life_9789264214262-en [Accessed 6 November 2023].

9 I. Watt (1957) *The Rise of the Novel: Studies in Defoe, Richardson, and Fielding*, Berkeley: University of California Press.

10 See R. Barthes (1977) The death of the author, in *Image, Music, Text*, translated by S. Heath, Hill & Wang. London: Fontana, pp 142–148; M. Foucault (2006) What is an

author?, in James D. Faubion (ed) *Aesthetics, Method, and Epistemology*, New York: New Press; M. Bakhtin (1997) *Problems of Dostoevsky's Poetics*, Minneapolis: University of Minnesota Press.

11 M. Bakhtin (1997) *Problems of Dostoevsky's Poetics*, Minneapolis: University of Minnesota Press.

12 J.D. Bolter (2001) *Writing Space*, New York: Routledge.

13 UNESCO Institute for Statistics Database and the United Nations (2020) *Literacy for Life, Work, Lifelong Learning and Education for Democracy: Report of the Secretary General (A/75/188)*, New York: UN, cited in United Nations Educational Scientific Organization (2021) *International Literacy Day 2021*, UNESCO [online]. Available at: https://en.unesco.org/sites/default/files/ild-2021-fact-sheet.pdf [Accessed 18 January 2023].

14 H. Rheingold (1993) *The Virtual Community: Homesteading on the Electronic Frontier*, New York: Perseus Books, p 36.

15 K.S. Goodman and P.H. Fries (2016) *Reading – the Grand Illusion: How and Why People Make Sense of Print*, New York: Routledge.

16 See L. Masterman (1980) *Teaching about Television*, New York: Palgrave; L. Masterman (1989) *Teaching the Media*, New York: Comedia.

17 Center for Media Literacy (2013) Len Masterman and the big ideas of media literacy. Available at: https://www.medialit.org/sites/default/files/connections/len-masterman-and-the-big-ideas-of-media-literacy.pdf [Accessed 13 January 2019].

18 L. Masterman (1995) 18 principles of media education, *Mediacy – Newsletter of Ontario's Association for Media Literacy*, 17(3), pp 2–4.

19 L. Masterman (1995) 18 principles of media education, *Mediacy – Newsletter of Ontario's Association for Media Literacy*, 17(3), pp 2–4.

20 R. Barthes (1957) *Mythologies*, translated by A. Lavers [1972], New York: Hill & Wang.

21 R. Hobbs (2016) *Exploring the Roots of Digital and Media Literacy through Personal Narrative*, Philadelphia: Temple University Press.

22 R. Barthes (1977) *Image-Music-Text: Roland Barthes*, translated by S. Heath, Glasgow: Collins, p 148.

23 R. Barthes (1977) *Image-Music-Text: Roland Barthes*, translated by S. Heath, Glasgow: Collins, p 148, emphasis in original.

24 R. Barthes (1975) *S/Z*, translated by R. Miller, New York: Hill & Wang.

25 L.M. Rosenblatt (1994) *The Reader, the Text, the Poem: The Transactional Theory of the Literary Work*, Carbondale: Southern Illinois University Press, p 169.

26 J. Katz (1998) Luring the lurkers, *Slashdot*. Available at: http://slashdot.org/features/98/12/28/1745252.shtml [Accessed 6 November 2023]. M. Muller (2012) Lurking as personal trait or situational disposition? Lurking and contributing in enterprise social media, *Proceedings of the ACM Conference on Computer-Supported Cooperative Work*, pp 253–256; J. Antin and C. Cheshire (2010) Readers are not free-riders: Reading as a form of participation on Wikipedia, *Proceedings of the 2010 ACM Conference on Computer-Supported Cooperative Work*. http://dx.doi.org/10.1145/1718918.1718942; B. Nonnecke, J. Preece, D. Andrews, and B. Voutour (2004) Online lurkers tell why they lurk, in paper presented at the 10th Americas conference on information systems, New York. Available at: http://www.cis.uoguelph.ca/~nonnecke/research/OnlineLurkersTellWhy.pdf [Accessed 6 November 2023].

27 G. Beenen, K. Ling, X. Wang, K. Chang, D. Frankowski, P. Resnick, and R.E. Kraut (2004) Using social psychology to motivate contributions to online communities. *Proceedings of the 2004 ACM Conference on Computer-Supported Cooperative Work (CSCW '04)*. doi:10.1145/1031607.1031642.

28 H. Jenkins, S. Ford, and J. Green (2018) *Spreadable Media: Creating Value and Meaning in a Networked Culture*, New York: New York University Press.

29 G. Hayes (2007) Web 2.0 and the myth of non-participation, *Personalize Media* [online]. Available at: https://www.personalizemedia.com/the-myth-of-non-participation-in-web-20-social-networks/ [Accessed 8 December 2022].

30 N. Ellison, P. Triệu, S. Schoenebeck, R. Brewer, and A. Israni (2020) Why we don't click: Interrogating the relationship between viewing and clicking in social media contexts by exploring the 'non-click', *Journal of Computer-Mediated Communication*, 25(6), pp 402–426.

31 L.M. Rosenblatt (2004) The transactional theory of reading and writing, in R.B. Ruddell and N.J. Unrau (eds) , 5th edition, Newark, DE: International Reading Association, Article 48, p 1367.

32 F. Saussure (1916) *Course in General Linguistics*, translated by W. Baskin [1959], New York: McGraw Hill.

33 C.S. Peirce (1931–1936) *The Collected Papers*, Volumes 1–6, edited by C. Hartshorne and P. Weiss, Cambridge, MA: Harvard University Press.

34 L.M. Rosenblatt (2004) The transactional theory of reading and writing, in R.B. Ruddell and N.J. Unrau (eds) *Theoretical Models and Processes of Reading*, 5th edition, Newark, DE: International Reading Association, Article 48, pp 1363–1398.

35 L.M. Rosenblatt (1969) Towards a transactional theory of reading, *Journal of Reading Behavior*, 1(1), pp 31–49.

36 K. Crenshaw (2014) *On Intersectionality: Essential Writings*, New York: New Press.

37 L. Rosenblatt (1995) Continuing the conversation: A clarification, *Research in the Teaching of English*, 29(3), pp 349–354.

38 I am choosing the word encounter rather than describing the event as the moment the eyes meet the page in an attempt to be inclusive of those whose disabilities require alternate ways of reading a text. For example, blind or visually impaired readers who utilize screen readers.

39 M. Knobel and C. Lankshear (2007) *A New Literacies Sampler*, New York: P. Lang.

40 D.E. Alvermann and R.K. Sanders (2019). Adolescent literacy in a digital world. *The International Encyclopedia of Media Literacy*, pp 1–6.

41 It is political organizations and the ways that they include state-sponsored education that seek to have limits on language. Think of monolingual policies or efforts to suppress reading lists or genre, etc. B.V. Street (2020) New literacies, new times: Developments in literacy studies, *Encyclopedia of Language and Education* [online], pp 418–431.

42 J. Sosnoski (1999). Hyper-readers and their reading engines. In G. Hawisher and C. Selfe (eds) *Passions, Pedagogies, and 21st Century Technologies*. Urbana: Utah State University Press, pp 161–177.

Chapter 3

1 Know Your Meme (2020) Conspiracy Keanu, *Know Your Meme* [online]. Available at: https://knowyourmeme.com/memes/conspiracy-keanu [Accessed 15 January 2023].

2 *Bill and Ted's Excellent Adventure* (1989) Orion Pictures, De Laurentiis Entertainment Group, Embassy Pictures.

3 Template varieties for Conspiracy Keanu can be found here: Imgflip (nd) Conspiracy Keanu meme generator, *Imgflip* [online]. Available at: https://imgflip.com/memegenerator/Conspiracy-Keanu [Accessed 16 January 2023].

4 D. Barton and M. Hamilton (1998) *Local Literacies: Reading and Writing in One Community*, London: Routledge; and B. Street (2003) What's 'new' in New Literacy Studies? Critical approaches to literacy in theory and practice, *Current Issues in Comparative Education*

[online], 5(2), pp 77–91. Available at: https://www.tc.columbia.edu/cice/pdf/25734_5_2_Street.pdf [Accessed 6 November 2023].

5   M. Hamilton (2000) Expanding the new literacy studies, in D. Barton, M. Hamilton and R. Ivanic (eds), *Situated Literacies: Reading and Writing in Context*, London: Routledge, pp 18.16–18.29.

6   S. Heath (1982) Protean shapes in literacy events, in D. Tannen (ed) *Spoken and Written Language: Exploring Orality and Literacy*, Norwood: Ablex, pp 91–118.

7   M. Hamilton (2000) Expanding the new literacy studies, in D. Barton, M. Hamilton and R. Ivanic (eds) *Situated Literacies: Reading and Writing in Context*, London: Routledge, pp 1816–1829.

8   E. Gross (2020) Underlying America's unrest is structural racism, *The Hill* [online]. Available at: https://thehill.com/opinion/civil-rights/500869-underlying-americas-unrest-is-structural-racism/ [Accessed 18 January 2023].

9   A. Costello (2012) Long Island Index releases study on school segregation. Long Island Herald [online]. Available at: https://www.liherald.com/stories/long-island-index-releases-study-on-school-segregation,40918 [Accessed 14 January 2023].

10 J. Kucsera and G. Orfield (2014) New York state's extreme segregation: Inequality, inaction, and a damaged future, *The Civil Rights Project* [online]. Los Angeles: UCLA. Available at: https://civilrightsproject.ucla.edu/research/k-12-education/integration-and-diversity/ny-norflet-report-placeholder/Kucsera-New-York-Extreme-Segregation-2014.pdf [Accessed 6 November 2023].

11 J.C. Mead (2003) Memories of segregation in Levittown, *The New York Times* [online] 11 May. Available at: https://www.nytimes.com/2003/05/11/nyregion/memories-of-segregation-in-levittown.html [Accessed 6 November 2023].

    United States Census (2021) Average household income US 69560, *United States Census Bureau* [online]. Available at: https://www.google.com/search?client=safari&rls=en&q=average+household+income+us+69560&ie=UTF-8&oe=UTF-8 [Accessed 16 January 2023].

12 M. Hicks (2010) Facebook tips: What's the difference between a Facebook page and group? *Facebook*, 24 February. Available at: https://www.facebook.com/notes/facebook/facebook-tips-whats-the-difference-between-a-facebook-page-and-group/324706977130/ [Accessed 6 November 2023].

13 B. Nonnecke and J. Preece (2003) Silent participants: Getting to know lurkers better, in C. Lueg and D. Fisher (eds) *From Usenet to CoWebs: Interacting with Social Information Spaces*, New York: Springer, pp 110–132.

14 B. Nonnecke, J. Preece, D. Andrews, and B. Voutour (2004) Online Lurkers tell why, in paper presented at the 10th Americas conference on information systems, New York. Available at: http://www.cis.uoguelph.ca/~nonnecke/research/OnlineLurkersTellWhy.pdf [Accessed 6 November 2023]; and B. Nonnecke, J. Preece, and D. Andrews (2004) What lurkers and posters think of each other, *Proceedings of the 37th Hawaii International Conference on System Science*. Available at: https://ieeexplore-ieee-org.ezproxy.hofstra.edu/stamp/stamp.jsp?tp=&arnumber=1265462 [Accessed 6 November 2023].

15 D. Coughlin and M. Brydon-Miller (2014) Community mapping, in D. Coughlin and M. Brydon-Miller (eds) *The SAGE Encyclopedia of Action Research*, London: SAGE.

16 *U.S. Constitution, Second Amendment*, Library of Congress. Available at: https://constitution.congress.gov/constitution/amendment-2/ [Accessed 14 March 2023].

17 S. Wineburg and S. McGrew (2019) Lateral reading and the nature of expertise: Reading less and learning more when evaluating digital information, *Teachers College Record: The Voice of Scholarship in Education*, 121(11), pp 1–40.

18   E. Lim, G.M. Sipley, L.S. Mohamed, F.B.T. Tripodi, and V. Perez (2021) Declarations of interdependence: How media literacy practices are developed, negotiated, rejected, and exploited across social media platforms, *AoIR Selected Papers of Internet Research*. https://doi.org/10.5210/spir.v2021i0.12298; G.M. Sipley (2020) 'Lurker' literacies: Living in/through neighborhood Facebook Groups, *AoIR Selected Papers of Internet Research*. https://doi.org/10.5210/spir.v2020i0.11331.

19   R. Rogers (2018) Otherwise engaged: Social media from vanity metrics to critical analytics, *International Journal of Communication*, 12, pp 450–472. Available at: https://dare.uva.nl/search?identifier=e7a7c11b-b199-4d7c-a9cb-fdf1dd74d493 [Accessed 20 February 2019].

20   J. Wortham (2012) Digital diary: Facebook poke and the tedium of success theater, *Bits Blog* [online]. Available at: https://bits.blogs.nytimes.com/2012/12/28/digital-diary-facebook-poke-and-the-tedium-of-success-theater/ [Accessed 15 January 2023].

21   A. Arad, O. Barzilay, and M. Perchick (2017) The impact of Facebook on social comparison and happiness: Evidence from a natural experiment, *SSRN Electronic Journal*. doi:10.2139/ssrn.2916158; and E. Kross, P. Verduyn, E. Demiralp, J. Park, D.S. Lee, N. Lin, H. Shablack, J. Jonides, and O. Ybarra (2013) Facebook use predicts declines in subjective well-being in young adults, *PLoS ONE* [online], 8(8).

22   National Endowment for the Arts (NEA) funding did increase during the years corresponding to Trump's presidency. President Trump tried several times to defund the NEA, but bipartisan congressional support sustained the organization and expanded its funding from US$149.8 million (2017) to US$162.3 million (2020). See G. Bowley (2021) Trump tried to end federal arts funding. Instead, it grew, *The New York Times*, 15 January. Available at: https://www.nytimes.com/2021/01/15/arts/trump-arts-nea-funding.html [Accessed 6 November 2023].

23   E. Wilbekin (2022) The fear of the hoodie, *The Cut* [online]. Available at: https://www.thecut.com/2022/01/trayvon-martin-hoodie-fear.html [Accessed 6 November 2023].

24   A. Lieb and L Lieb (Hosts). (2020). Real estate opportunities by location in 2020 and 2021. (No. 49, 17 May). In *The LIEB Cast*. Available at: https://www.listentolieb.com/876124/3756257-real-estate-opportunities-by-location-in-2020-and-2021 [Accessed 6 November 2023]

25   A. Lieb and L. Lieb (Hosts). (2020). Real estate opportunities by location in 2020 and 2021 (No. 49, 17 May). In *The LIEB Cast*. Available at: https://www.listentolieb.com/876124/3756257-real-estate-opportunities-by-location-in-2020-and-2021 [Accessed 6 November 2023].

26   A. Lieb and L. Lieb (Hosts). (2020, May 17). Real estate opportunities by location in 2020 and 2021 (No. 49, 17 May). In *The LIEB Cast*. Available at: https://www.listentolieb.com/876124/3756257-real-estate-opportunities-by-location-in-2020-and-2021 [Accessed 6 November 2023].

27   M. Popovac and C. Fullwood (2019) The psychology of online lurking, in A. Attrill-Smith, C. Fullwood, M. Keep, and D.J. Kuss (eds) *The Oxford Handbook of Cyberpsychology*, Oxford: Oxford University Press, pp 285–305; and J. Preece, B. Nonnecke, and D. Andrews (2004) The top five reasons for lurking: Improving community experiences for everyone, *Computers in Human Behavior*, 20(2), pp 201–223..

28   A. Giddens (2013) *Modernity and Self-Identity: Self and Society in the Late Modern Age*, Hoboken: Wiley; and A. Giddens (1990) *The Consequences of Modernity*, Redwood City, CA: Stanford University Press, p 64.

29   J. Dewey (1933) *How We Think: A Restatement of the Relation of Reflective Thinking to the Educative Process*, Boston: Houghton Mifflin.

30   After Amazon's decision to remove offensive and sexist merchandise, including T-shirts with the phrase 'Vote Joe and the Ho' sold by third-party providers, the 'Vote Joe and

the Ho' memes quickly disappeared. See C. Duffy (2020) Amazon removes vulgar anti-Biden and Harris shirts, *CNN* [online]. Available at: https://www.cnn.com/2020/08/19/tech/amazon-removes-anti-biden-products/index.html [Accessed 6 November 2023]. The meme from my research can be found in my dissertation: G. Sipley (2021) *Literacy Practices of Lurkers in Facebook Groups.* [Dissertation]. Hofstra University.

Chapter 4

1   S. Tibbette (2018) *Condescending Wonka/creepy Wonka, Know Your Meme* [online]. Available at: https://knowyourmeme.com/memes/condescending-wonka-creepy-wonka [Accessed 14 January 2023].

2   *Willy Wonka and the Chocolate Factory* (1971) Wolper Pictures.

3   *Willy Wonka and the Chocolate Factory* (1971) Wolper Pictures.

4   Scholars who study lurking have routinely cited learning communities and health-based communities as places where lurking is beneficial. For an overview of sources see M. Popovac and C. Fullwood (2019) The psychology of online lurking, in A. Attrill-Smith, C. Fullwood, M. Keep, and D.J. Kuss (eds) *The Oxford Handbook of Cyberpsychology*, Oxford: Oxford University Press, pp 285–305.

5   A. Correal (2016) Pantsuit Nation, a 'secret' Facebook hub, celebrates Clinton, *The New York Times* [online] 8 November. Available at: https://www.nytimes.com/2016/11/09/us/politics/facebook-pantsuit-nation-clinton.html [Accessed 8 December 2022].

6   N. Woolf (2016) 'Nasty woman': Trump attacks Clinton during final debate, *The Guardian* [online] 20 October. Available at: https://www.theguardian.com/us-news/2016/oct/20/nasty-woman-donald-trump-hillary-clinton [Accessed 8 December 2022].

7   D. Chugh (2018) *Person You Mean to Be: Confronting Bias to Build a Better Workplace and World*, New York: HarperCollins.

8   L. Michelle (2022) *The White Allies Handbook*, New York: Dafina.

9   Food and Nutrition Service (2021) SNAP retailer reminder: Allowable items, *Food and Nutrition Service* [online] 26 October. Available at: https://www.fns.usda.gov/snap/snap-retailer-reminder-ineligibles [Accessed 14 March 2023]; and Food and Nutrition Service (2022) WIC frequently asked questions (FAQs), *Food and Nutrition Service* [online] 2 August. Available at: https://www.fns.usda.gov/wic/frequently-asked-questions [Accessed 6 November 2023].

10 M. Popovac and C. Fullwood (2019) The psychology of online lurking, in A. Attrill-Smith, C. Fullwood, M. Keep, and D.J. Kuss (eds) *The Oxford Handbook of Cyberpsychology*, Oxford: Oxford University Press, pp 285–305; C.F. van Uden-Kraan, C.H. Drossaert, E. Taal, B.R. Shaw, E.R. Seydel, and M.A. van de Laar (2008) Empowering processes and outcomes of participation in online support groups for patients with breast cancer, arthritis, or fibromyalgia, *Qualitative Health Research*, 18(3), pp 405–417; C. Fullwood, D. Chadwick, M. Keep, A. Attrill-Smith, T. Asbury, and G. Kirwan (2019) Lurking towards empowerment: Explaining propensity to engage with online health support groups and its association with positive outcomes, *Computers in Human Behavior*, 90, pp 131–140; J. Preece, B. Nonnecke, and D. Andrews (2004) The top five reasons for lurking: Improving community experiences for everyone, *Computers in Human Behavior*, 20(2), pp 201–223.

11 S. Fox and M. Duggan (2013) Part two: Sources of health information, *Pew Research Center: Internet, Science & Tech* [online]. Available at: https://www.pewresearch.org/internet/2013/11/26/part-two-sources-of-health-information/ [Accessed 8 December 2022].

12 See J.Y. Han, J. Hou, E. Kim, and D.H. Gustafson (2013) Lurking as an active participation process: A longitudinal investigation of engagement with an online cancer support group, *Health Communication*, 29(9), pp 911–923; and J. Preece, B. Nonnecke, and D. Andrews

(2004) The top five reasons for lurking: Improving community experiences for everyone, *Computers in Human Behavior*, 20(2), pp 201–223.

13 C. Fullwood, D. Chadwick, M. Keep, A. Attrill-Smith, T. Asbury, and G. Kirwan (2019) Lurking towards empowerment: Explaining propensity to engage with online health support groups and its association with positive outcomes, *Computers in Human Behavior*, 90, pp 131–140.

14 C. Fullwood, D. Chadwick, M. Keep, A. Attrill-Smith, T. Asbury, and G. Kirwan (2019) Lurking towards empowerment: Explaining propensity to engage with online health support groups and its association with positive outcomes, *Computers in Human Behavior*, 90, pp 131–140, at p 131.

15 C. Fullwood, D. Chadwick, M. Keep, A. Attrill-Smith, T. Asbury, and G. Kirwan (2019) Lurking towards empowerment: Explaining propensity to engage with online health support groups and its association with positive outcomes, *Computers in Human Behavior*, 90, pp 131–140, at p 131.

16 Studies in healthcare use sensemaking as one word, whereas internet-based studies of healthcare tend to use it as a singular term. See E.M. Goering and A. Krause (2018) From sense making to decision making when living with cancer, *Communication & Medicine*, 14(3), pp 268–273; A.B. Anderson (2019) It doesn't make sense, but we do: Framing disease in an online metastatic breast cancer support community, *Qualitative Research in Medicine and Healthcare*, 3(2); and A. Anderson (2019) *Walking Each Other Home: Sensemaking of Illness Identity in an Online Metastatic Cancer Community*. Dissertation, University of South Florida. https://digitalcommons.usf.edu/cgi/viewcontent.cgi?article=9200&context= etd [Accessed 6 November 2023].

17 C.W. Choo and N. Bontis (2002) *The Strategic Management of Intellectual Capital and Organizational Knowledge*, New York: Oxford University Press; and C.W. Choo (2001) *Sensemaking, Knowledge Creation, and Decision Making* [online]. Available at: http://choo. fis.utoronto.ca/OUP/chooOUP/ [Accessed 8 December 2022].

18 K.A. O'Brien (2018) I can't jump ship from Facebook yet, *The New York Times* [online] 14 April. Available at: https://www.nytimes.com/2018/04/14/opinion/sunday/delete-facebook-parenting-special-needs.html [Accessed 15 January 2023].

19 J.T. Child and S.C. Starcher (2016) Fuzzy Facebook privacy boundaries: Exploring mediated lurking, vague-booking, and Facebook privacy management, *Computers in Human Behavior*, 54, pp 483–490.

20 Mediated lurking of romantic partners and close relations has been studied by B. McEwan (2013) Sharing, caring, and surveilling: An actor–partner interdependence model examination of Facebook relational maintenance strategies, *Cyberpsychology, Behavior, and Social Networking*, 16(12), pp 863–869; D. Trottier (2012) Interpersonal surveillance on social media, *Canadian Journal of Communication* [online], 37(2); and A. Lee and P.S. Cook (2014) The conditions of exposure and immediacy: Internet surveillance and Generation Y, *Journal of Sociology*, 51(3), pp 674–688.

21 L. Hammond Gerido (2022) Interview with Lynette Hammond Gerido, 20 May 2022, Zoom.

22 A. Downing (2019) Our cancer support group on Facebook is trapped, *Medium* [online]. Available at: https://tincture.io/our-cancer-support-group-on-facebook-is-trapped-f2030 a3c7c71 [Accessed 14 January 2023].

23 The Light Collective (2020) Peer support group: Moderation best practices, *The Light Collective* [online]. Available at: https://lightcollective.org/wp-content/uploads/ 2020/11/Online-Peer-Support-Moderation-Best-Practices-Final-2.pdf [Accessed 8 December 2022].

24 J. Constine (2022) Facebook changes mission statement to 'bring the world closer together', *TechCrunch* [online]. Available at: https://techcrunch.com/2017/06/22/bring-the-world-closer-together/?guccounter=1&guce_referrer=aHR0cHM6Ly93d3cuZ29vZ2xlLmNvbS8&guce_referrer_sig=AQAAAAK-aAsbLkpIL07n52AVcuE5_5MIF3WEV37kGY5yuS9z4MPmSYz3qc_wM-SNacvnvMe14k1915pQ4PM1e6-3F_XvUzClaNnPKqyg9cwjNhryR5IqM1lX8NGWe2fUNor94ScmbFMFI5muBjTl7UvkFlORSNq136YkPPFBukzNXcRG [Accessed 14 January 2023].

25 Facebook (2020) We're launching new engagement features, ways to discover groups and more tools for admins, *Facebook Community* [online]. Available at: https://www.facebook.com/community/whats-new/facebook-communities-summit-keynote-recap/ [Accessed 14 January 2023].

26 V. Elliott (2023) TikTok and Meta's moderators form a united front in Germany, *Wired* [online] 13 March. Available at: https://www.wired.com/story/tiktok-and-metas-moderators-form-a-united-front-in-germany/ [Accessed 18 March 2023].

27 S.T. Roberts (2019) *Behind the Screen*, New Haven: Yale University Press, p 209.

Chapter 5

1 Imgur (2020) Surely I'm not the only one …, *Imgur* [online]. Available at: https://imgur.com/gallery/vDsfgzX [Accessed 14 January 2023].

2 K.S. Goodman and E. Clearinghouse (1981) *Miscue Analysis: Applications to Reading Instruction*, Urbana: Ncte.

3 Many US companies traditionally offer two weeks paid vacation; however, workers are often encouraged and rewarded for not taking the full time. In an economy where there is much precarity and gig work, it is challenging to find positions that will even offer the corporate base of two weeks. There is a move towards more flexible vacation time particularly with the ability for a greater number of workers to perform their roles remotely, but this does not apply to the vast majority of US workers. See the *Harvard Business Review* article that inspired a lot of think pieces in US media about this pre-pandemic: N. Pasricha and S. Nigam (2017) What one company learned from forcing employees to use their vacation time, *Harvard Business Review* [online]. Available at: https://hbr.org/2017/08/what-one-company-learned-from-forcing-employees-to-use-their-vacation-time [Accessed 6 November 2023].

4 K.S. Goodman and Y.M. Goodman (2014) *Making Sense of Learners Making Sense of Written Language*, New York: Routledge.

5 Meme Generator (nd) How can you read this? There's no pictures! *memegenerator.net* [online]. Available at: https://memegenerator.net/instance/72375234/gaston-reading-how-can-you-read-this-theres-no-pictures [Accessed 14 January 2023].

6 Know Your Meme (2023) The more you know: Image gallery (list view), *Know Your Meme* [online]. Available at: https://knowyourmeme.com/memes/the-more-you-know/photos [Accessed 14 January 2023].

7 K. Goodman, P.H. Fries, and S.L. Strauss (2016) *Reading – the Grand Illusion: How and Why People Make Sense of Print*, New York: Routledge.

8 K. Goodman, P.H. Fries, and S.L. Strauss (2016) *Reading – the Grand Illusion: How and Why People Make Sense of Print*, New York: Routledge.

9 National Center for Education Statistics (2018) Exhibit 1. Description of PISA reading literacy proficiency levels: 2018, *National Center for Education Statistics* [online]. Available at: https://nces.ed.gov/surveys/pisa/pisa2018/pdf/ReadingProfLevelDescriptionV2.pdf [Accessed 14 January 2023].

10 Reading Recovery, an early intervention national literacy programme developed by Marie Clay in New Zealand in the 1970s, was adopted by schools in Australia, Canada,

Europe, and the United States in the 1980s. Irene Fountas and Gay Su Pinnell built upon Clay's work to create a levelled literacy intervention system more popularly known as Fountas and Pinnell's levelled reading that tiers books to grade levels and in the late 1990s developed a robust catalogue of books and curricular materials targeted to each tier, which continue to be purchased by schools and families worldwide. Other commercial-oriented educational endeavours, most notably by Lucy Calkins' Columbia University Teachers College Reading and Writing Workshop, produce additional goods and services that integrate Fountas and Pinnell. Cognitive scientists have disproven the basic tenets of Clay's work and by extension the work of Fountas and Pinnell and Calkins. Despite the concerns raised by scholars, levelled literacy products continue to be sold worldwide by their publisher, Heinemann. This Reading Recovery Community (nd) *International Connections*, Reading Recovery Council of North America [online]. Available at: https://readingrecovery.org/reading-recovery/training/international-connections/ [Accessed 14 January 2023]; Fountas and Pinnell Literacy (2023) *Fountas and Pinnell Information and Teacher Community*, Fountas and Pinnell [online]. Available at: https://www.fountasandpinnell.com [Accessed 6 November 2023]. The Reading and Writing Project: Teachers College Columbia University (2023) *Teachers College Reading and Writing Project*, readingandwritingproject.org [online]. Available at: https://readingandwritingproject.org [Accessed 14 January 2023].

[11] Y.M. Goodman, D.J. Watson, and C.L. Burke (2005) *Reading Miscue Inventory: From Evaluation to Instruction*, Katonah: Richard C. Owen Publishers.

[12] Y.M. Goodman, D.J. Watson, and C.L. Burke (2005) *Reading Miscue Inventory: From Evaluation to Instruction*, Katonah: Richard C. Owen Publishers.

[13] K.S. Goodman and Y.M. Goodman (2014) *Making Sense of Learners Making Sense of Written Language*, New York: Routledge.

[14] d. boyd (2018) What hath we wrought? *danah boyd SXSW EDU Keynote* [online]. Available at: https://www.youtube.com/watch?time_continue=16&v=0I7FVyQCjNg [Accessed 13 January 2023].

[15] W.J. Potter (2010) The state of media literacy, *Journal of Broadcasting & Electronic Media*, 54(4), pp 675–696.

[16] W.J. Potter (2010) The state of media literacy, *Journal of Broadcasting & Electronic Media*, 54(4), pp 675–696, at p 679.

[17] R. Hobbs (2011) The state of media literacy: A response to Potter, *Journal of Broadcasting & Electronic Media*, 55(3), pp 419–430, at p 420.

[18] W.J. Potter (2022) Analysis of definitions of media literacy, *Journal of Media Literacy Education*, 14(2), pp 27–43. Potter writes: 'There are some scholars who believe that there is a high degree of agreement about what media literacy means (Aufderheide, 1997; Livingstone, 2003; Redmond, 2012; Scharrer, 2009; Scharrer & Cooks 2006; Schmidt, 2013; Torrent, 2011). there are other scholars who claim that there is great diversity in what people mean when they use the term (Brown, 1998; Christ, 2004; Fedorov 2003; Hobbs & Jensen 2009; Iaquinto & Keeler, 2012; Lantela, 2019; Maksl, Ashley, & Craft, 2015; Martens, 2010; Palsa & Ruokamo, 2015; Potter 2010; Rogow, 2004). Perceptions of diversity of meaning are not limited to the United States but instead seem to be the case globally (Hipeli, 2019; Parola & Ranieri, 2010; Zylka, Müller, & Martins, 2011).

[19] W.J. Potter (2022) Analysis of definitions of media literacy, *Journal of Media Literacy Education*, 14(2), pp 27–43.

[20] W.J. Potter (2022) Analysis of definitions of media literacy, *Journal of Media Literacy Education*, 14(2), pp 27–43.

[21] D. Kellner and J. Share (2005) Toward critical media literacy: Core concepts, debates, organizations, and policy, *Discourse: Studies in the Cultural Politics of Education*, 26(3), pp 369–386.

22 D. Kellner and J. Share (2005) Toward critical media literacy: Core concepts, debates, organizations, and policy, *Discourse: Studies in the Cultural Politics of Education*, 26(3), pp 369–386.

23 R. Hobbs (1998) The seven great debates in the media literacy movement, *Journal of Communication*, 48(1), pp 16–32; and R. Hobbs (2011) The state of media literacy: A response to Potter, *Journal of Broadcasting & Electronic Media*, 55(3), pp 419–430.

24 R. Hobbs (2011) The state of media literacy: A response to Potter, *Journal of Broadcasting & Electronic Media*, 55(3), pp 419–430.

25 D. Kellner and J. Share (2005) Toward critical media literacy: Core concepts, debates, organizations, and policy, *Discourse: Studies in the Cultural Politics of Education*, 26(3), pp 369–386, at p 377.

26 D. Kellner and J. Share (2005) Toward critical media literacy: Core concepts, debates, organizations, and policy, *Discourse: Studies in the Cultural Politics of Education*, 26(3), pp 369–386, at p 377.

27 National Association for Media Literacy Education (2015) About NAMLE, 11 April. Available at: https://namle.net/about-namle/namles-history/ [Accessed 13 January 2019].

28 Action Coalition for Media Education (nd) Mission and vision. Available at: https://acmesmartmediaeducation.net/ [Accessed 13 January 2019].

29 National Association for Media Literacy Education (2007) Core principles of media literacy education in the United States. Available at: https://namle.net/publications/core-principles/ [Accessed 6 November 2023].

30 D.C. Moore and E. Bonilla (2014) Media literacy education and the common core state standards. Available at: https://namleboard.files.wordpress.com/2015/04/namlemleccssguide.pdf [Accessed 13 January 2019].

31 W.J. Potter (2010) The state of media literacy, *Journal of Broadcasting & Electronic Media*, 54(4), pp 675–696, at p 679.

32 See D. Adams and M. Hamm (2001) *Literacy in a Multimedia Age*, Norwood: Christopher-Gordon Publishers; D.E. Alvermann, J.S. Moon, and M.C. Hagood (1999) *Popular Culture in the Classroom: Teaching and Researching Critical Media Literacy*, Newark, DE: International Reading Association; J.A. Brown (1991) *Television 'Critical Viewing Skills' Education: Major Media Literacy Projects in the United States and Selected Countries*, Hillsdale: Lawrence Erlbaum Associates; M. Mackey (2007) *Literacies across Media*, 2nd edn, New York: Routledge; P. Messaris (1998) Visual aspects of media literacy, *Journal of Communication*, 48(1), pp 70–80; D. Sholle and S. Denski (1994) *Media Education and the (Re)Production of Culture*, Westport: Bergin & Garvey; and A. Silverblatt, J. Ferry, and B. Finan (1999) *Approaches to Media Literacy: A Handbook*, Armonk: M.E. Sharpe.

33 See J. Meyrowitz (1998) Multiple media literacies, *Journal of Communication*, 48(1), pp 96–108; R. Pattison (1982) *On Literacy: The Politics of the Word from Homer to the Age of Rock*, Oxford: Oxford University Press; A. Silverblatt (1995) *Media Literacy: Keys to Interpreting Media Messages*, Westport: Praeger; H. Zettl (1998) Contextual media aesthetics as the basis for media literacy, *Journal of Communication*, 48(1), pp 81–95.

34 See C. Bazalgette (1997) An agenda for the second phase of media literacy development, in R. Kubey (ed) *Media Literacy in the Information Age: Current Perspectives, Information and Behavior*, Volume 6, New Brunswick: Transaction Publishers, pp 69–78; R. Hobbs (1996) Media literacy, media activism, *Telemedium, The Journal of Media Literacy*, 42(3), p iii; and W.J. Potter (2004) *Theory of Media Literacy: A Cognitive Approach*, Thousand Oaks: SAGE.

35 P. Mihailidis (2008) Are we speaking the same language? Assessing the state of media literacy in U.S. higher education, *SIMILE: Studies in Media & Information Literacy Education*, 8(4), pp 1–14.

[36] M. Payne and J.R. Barbera (2013) *A Dictionary of Cultural and Critical Theory*, Malden, MA: Wiley-Blackwell, p 313.

[37] R. Hobbs (2011) The state of media literacy: A response to Potter, *Journal of Broadcasting & Electronic Media*, 55(3), pp 419–430, at p 423.

[38] P. Mihailidis (2008) Are we speaking the same language? Assessing the state of media literacy in U.S. higher education, *SIMILE: Studies in Media & Information Literacy Education*, 8(4), pp 1–14.

[39] M. Bulger and P. Davison (2018) *The Promises, Challenges, and Futures of Media Literacy*, Data & Society [online]. Available at: https://datasociety.net/library/the-promises-challenges-and-futures-of-media-literacy/ [Accessed 6 November 2023].

[40] E. Lim, G.M. Sipley, L.S. Mohamed, F.B.T. Tripodi, and V. Perez (2021) Declarations of interdependence: How media literacy practices are developed, negotiated, rejected, and exploited across social media platforms, *AoIR Selected Papers of Internet Research*. doi:10.5210/spir.v2021i0.12298.

[41] Pinterest and Etsy are two sites where 'Reading is a Window to the World' merchandise abounds. Some of these products are attributed to novelist Lyn Butler. The phrase, 'Reading is a Window to the World' is a sentiment that appears in slight variations across posters, T-shirts, notebooks, and other merchandise marketed to young children and the teachers who guide them.

[42] Within the first financial quarter of 2023, Barnes & Noble reported record financial gains by prioritizing book sales. It will be interesting to track whether this renewed focus on bookselling will persist in coming financial quarters. See M. Hiltzik (2023) Barnes & Noble saved itself by putting books first. Imagine that, *Los Angeles Times* [online] 1 February. Available at: https://www.latimes.com/business/story/2023-02-01/barnes-noble-survived-a-near-death-experience-and-its-now-growing-again [Accessed 6 November 2023].

[43] See F. Douglass, J.R. Mckivigan, P.P. Hinks, and H.L. Kaufman (2016) *Narrative of the Life of Frederick Douglass, an American Slave, Written by Himself*, New Haven: Yale University Press.

[44] history.house.gov (nd) Suffrage for 18-year-olds, *US House of Representatives: History, Art & Archives* [online]. Available at: https://history.house.gov/Records-and-Research/Listing/c_016/ [Accessed 6 November 2023].

[45] The world literacy rankings look beyond standardized assessment and holistically include the newspaper circulation, internet and library availability, years of schooling, and the number of bookstores. See J.W. Miller and M.C. McKenna (2016) *World Literacy*, New York: Routledge. A quick overview of Iceland's unique literacy culture can be found in A. Twomey (2016) Iceland: A country of bibliophiles, *Book Riot* [online]. Available at: https://bookriot.com/iceland-a-country-of-bibliophiles/#:~:text=Perhaps%20due%20to%20their%20geographical [Accessed 12 January 2023]. Iceland is also not an isolated example. Other Nordic nations like Finland as well as Japan regularly rank highly.

[46] UNESCO Institute for Statistics and Global Education Monitoring Report Team (2017) *Reducing Global Poverty through Universal Primary and Secondary Education*, Unesco.org [online]. Available at: https://unesdoc.unesco.org/ark:/48223/pf0000250392 [Accessed 12 January 2023].

[47] W. Shakespeare, W.H. Sherman, and P. Hulme (2004) *The Tempest: Sources and Contexts, Criticism, Rewritings and Appropriations*, New York: Norton.

[48] W. Shakespeare, W.H. Sherman, and P. Hulme (2004) *The Tempest: Sources and Contexts, Criticism, Rewritings and Appropriations*, New York: Norton.

[49] B. Ashcroft (2009) *Caliban's Voice*, New York: Routledge.

[50] G. Spivak (2010) *Can the Subaltern Speak? Reflections on the History of an Idea*, New York: Columbia University Press.

51 A. Karuza (2022) Council post: Make the most of the creator economy, *Forbes* [online]. Available at: https://www.forbes.com/sites/theyec/2022/07/18/make-the-most-of-the-creator-economy/?sh=1cebe99f16e9 [Accessed 12 January 2023].

52 B.E. Duffy (2018) *(Not) Getting Paid to Do What You Love: Gender, Social Media, and Aspirational Work*, New Haven: Yale University Press.

53 More recent studies show that although the pay gap for Black macroinfluencers is widening, it is narrowing for Black microinfluencers. See S. Bishop (2021) Influencer management tools: Algorithmic cultures, brand safety, and bias, *Social Media + Society*, 7(1), 205630512110030; A. Pei, Y. Bart, K. Pauwels, and K. Chan (2022) Racial pay gap in influencer marketing, *papers.ssrn.com* [online]. Available at: https://papers.ssrn.com/sol3/papers.cfm?abstract_id=4156872 [Accessed 10 November 2022]; and MSL (2021) MSL study reveals racial pay gap in influencer marketing, *www.prnewswire.com* [online]. Available at: https://www.prnewswire.com/news-releases/msl-study-reveals-racial-pay-gap-in-influencer-marketing-301437451.html?tc=eml_cleartime [Accessed 6 November 2023].

54 W. Safire (2009) Pay-to-play, *The New York Times* [online] 3 March. Available at: https://www.nytimes.com/2009/03/08/magazine/08wwln-safire-t.html [Accessed 11 January 2023].

55 See J. Zote (2019) 65 social media statistics to bookmark in 2019. Available at: https://sproutsocial.com/insights/social-media-statistics/; and L.H. Ferreira (2019) Does organic content still work on social media? 15 March. Available at: https://www.socialbakers.com/blog/marketer-luigi-henrique-ferreira-organic-social-media-content, cited in K.R. Place and E. Ciszek (2021) Troubling dialogue and digital media: A subaltern critique, *Social Media + Society*, 7(1), 205630512098444.

56 Ali, C. (2021) *Farm Fresh Broadband the Politics of Rural Connectivity*. Cambridge, MA: MIT Press.

57 J. Lanier (2018) *Ten Arguments for Deleting Your Social Media Accounts Right Now*, London: Random House.

58 E. Johnson (2018) If you can quit social media, but don't, then you're part of the problem, Jaron Lanier says, *Vox* [online]. Available at: https://www.vox.com/2018/7/27/17618756/jaron-lanier-deleting-social-media-book-kara-swisher-too-embarrassed-podcast [Accessed 8 December 2022].

59 E. Johnson (2018) If you can quit social media, but don't, then you're part of the problem, Jaron Lanier says, *Vox* [online]. Available at: https://www.vox.com/2018/7/27/17618756/jaron-lanier-deleting-social-media-book-kara-swisher-too-embarrassed-podcast [Accessed 8 December 2022].

60 R.J. So and G. Wezerek (2020) Just how white is the book industry? *The New York Times* [online] 11 December. Available at: https://www.nytimes.com/interactive/2020/12/11/opinion/culture/diversity-publishing-industry.html [Accessed 6 November 2023].

61 The 2019 Authors Guild survey finds that the median author income for part-time authors in the United States is US$6,250, for full-time authors it is US$20,300 This salary is drastically below the US median earnings for both families and individuals. Author income is not exclusively from book sales. Authors must also earn income through speaking engagements, book reviewing, and teaching – gigs that require a social media presence to obtain. See: S. Nicolas (2021) How much do authors make per book? *Book Riot* [online]. Available at: https://bookriot.com/how-much-do-authors-make-per-book/ [Accessed 11 January 2023]; A. Renard (2022) How to make money through social media without being an influencer, *Jane Friedman* [online]. Available at: https://www.janefriedman.com/make-money-through-social-media/ [Accessed 11 January 2023].

62 A. Brock (2020) *Distributed Blackness: African American Cybercultures*, New York: New York University Press, p 5.

63 S.U. Noble (2018) *Algorithms of Oppression: How Search Engines Reinforce Racism*, New York: New York University Press, p 175.

64 Camri Policy Briefs and Reports (2018) Misinformation policy in sub-Saharan Africa: From laws and regulations to media literacy [online]. Available at: https://libr ary.oapen.org/viewer/web/viewer.html?file=/bitstream/handle/20.500.12657/50175/ 9781914386053.pdf?sequence=1&isAllowed=y [Accessed 8 December 2022].

65 D.O. Vicol (2020) Who is most likely to believe and to share misinformation? *Full Fact*. Available at: https://fullfact.org/media/uploads/who-believes-shares-misinformation.pdf [Accessed 6 November 2023].

66 See N. Tannous, P. Belesiotis, N. Tchakarian, and R. Stewart (2019) Public engagement with politics, information and news – Nigeria, *Africa Check* [online]. Available at: http:// africacheck.org/how-to-fact-check/fact-checking-studies [Accessed 8 December 2022]; and S. Kolawole and E. Umejei (2018) Nigeria, *Media Landscapes* [online]. Available at: http://medialandscapes.org/country/nigeria [Accessed 8 December 2022].

67 I. Aguadad, Y. Sandoval-Romero, and R. Rosell (2016) Media literacy from international organizations in Europe and Latin America. *Journal of Media Literacy*. Available at: https:// www.researchgate.net/publication/305475789_Media_literacy_from_international_ organizations_in_Europe_and_Latin_America [Accessed 6 November 2023].

68 D.O. Vicol (2020) Who is most likely to believe and to share misinformation? *Full Fact*. Available at: https://fullfact.org/media/uploads/who-believes-shares-misinformation.pdf [Accessed 6 November 2023].

69 R. Morduchowicz (2017) Media literacy in Latin America: The Argentine experience, in B. De Abreu, P. Mihailidis, A. Lee, J. Melki, and J. McDougall (eds) *International Handbook of Media Literacy Education*, New York: Routledge, pp 33–42.

70 S. Roy (2017) Significance of media literacy education in India, *International Journal of Education & Applied Sciences Research*, 4(3), 1–8.

71 Camri Policy Briefs and Reports (2018) Misinformation policy in sub-Saharan Africa: From laws and regulations to media literacy [online]. Available at: https://libr ary.oapen.org/viewer/web/viewer.html?file=/bitstream/handle/20.500.12657/50175/ 9781914386053.pdf?sequence=1&isAllowed=y [Accessed 8 December 2022].

72 UNESCO (2013) Global media and information literacy assessment framework: Country read-iness and competencies, *UNESCO*. Available at: https://unesdoc.unesco.org/ark:/ 48223/pf0000224655 [Accessed 6 November 2023].

73 See A. Fedorov and A. Levitskaya (2019) Media literacy in Russia, in *The International Encyclopedia of Media Literacy*, Hoboken, NJ: Wiley, pp 1–7; I.A. Bykov and M.V. Medvedeva (2020) Media literacy in the system of the secondary education in Russia, *Espacios*, 41(48), pp 393–401; and A. Fedorov (2015) Russian media education literacy centers in the 21st century, *The Journal of Media Literacy*, 57(1&2).

74 There are costs associated with the in-person National Association for Media Literacy Association conferences, but there is often free or reduced pricing for virtual events. See National Association for Media Literacy Education (2020) Events, *NAMLE* [online]. Available at: https://namle.net/events/ [Accessed 11 January 2023].

75 This issue is not exclusive to media literacy. Teachers in the United States pay out-of-pocket for most of their own resources and tangible supplies. The US government offers a small federal tax deduction of US$250 to teachers in acknowledgement of these additional costs. See Internal Revenue Service (2022) Topic no. 458 educator expense deduction, *Internal Revenue Service* [online]. Available at: https://www.irs.gov/taxtopics/ tc458 [Accessed 8 December 2022].

[76] Media Smarts: Canada's Centre For Digital And Media Literacy (2012) What we do, *MediaSmarts* [online]. Available at: https://mediasmarts.ca/about-us/what-we-do [Accessed 8 December 2022].

[77] Australian Media Literacy Alliance (2022) Australian Media Literacy Alliance research reveals urgent need for a national media literacy strategy, *Australian Media Literacy Alliance* [online]. Available at: https://medialiteracy.org.au/australian-media-literacy-alliance-research-reveals-urgent-need-for-a-national-media-literacy-strategy-3/ [Accessed 8 December 2022].

[78] T. Notely, S. Chambers, S. Park, and M. Dezuanni (2021) Adult media literacy in Australia: Attitudes, experiences and needs, *Western Sydney University* [online]. Available at: https://www.westernsydney.edu.au/__data/assets/pdf_file/0007/1824640/Australian_adult_media_literacy_report_2021.pdf [Accessed 11 January 2023].

[79] Australian Media Literacy Alliance (2022) Australian Media Literacy Alliance research reveals urgent need for a national media literacy strategy, *Australian Media Literacy Alliance* [online]. Available at: https://medialiteracy.org.au/australian-media-literacy-alliance-research-reveals-urgent-need-for-a-national-media-literacy-strategy-3/ [Accessed 8 December 2022].

[80] UNESCO (2022) There is still no unifying idea for adult education in the digital age, *Institute for Lifelong Learning* [online]. Available at: https://www.uil.unesco.org/en/articles/there-still-no-unifying-idea-adult-education-digital-age?hub=39 [Accessed 8 December 2022].

[81] L.M. Siad (2022) Interview with Ladan Mohammad Siad, 8 August, Zoom.

[82] L.M. Siad (2022) Interview with Ladan Mohammad Siad, 8 August, Zoom.

[83] L. Russell (2020) *GLITCH FEMINISM: A Manifesto*, s.l.: Verso.

[84] L. Russell (2020) *GLITCH FEMINISM: A Manifesto*, s.l.: Verso.

[85] NAMLE (2019) Snapshot 2019: The state of media literacy education in the United States, *NAMLE* [online]. Available at: https://namle.net/wp-content/uploads/2020/10/SOML_FINAL.pdf [Accessed 7 December 2022].

[86] d. boyd (2018) What hath we wrought? *danah boyd SXSW EDU Keynote* [online]. Available at: https://www.youtube.com/watch?time_continue=16&v=0I7FVyQCjNg [Accessed 13 January 2023].

[87] E. Lim (2021) #DefundThePolice – Black Lives Matter: Radical algorithmic literacy, *AoIR Selected Papers of Internet Research, 2021*. https://doi.org/10.5210/spir.v2021i0.12298.

[88] This strategy is outlined in the report by the 21st Century Working Group (New Zealand) (2014) Future-focused learning in connected communities, *New Zealand Ministry of Education* [online]. Available at: https://d1pf6s1cgoc6y0.cloudfront.net/7f9576aea1a44 4409cf972003a6cb5e9.pdf [Accessed 6 November 2023]. Applications of this report can be found at the National Library of New Zealand (nd) Digital literacy and the New Zealand curriculum [online]. Available at: https://natlib.govt.nz/schools/digital-literacy/unders tanding-digital-literacy/digital-literacy-and-the-new-zealand-curriculum [Accessed 11 January 2023].

[89] C. Michael (2019) *SIFT (The Four Moves)*, Hapgood [online]. Available at: https://hapg ood.us/2019/06/19/sift-the-four-moves/ [Accessed 7 December 2022].

[90] See A. Quan-Haase and A.L. Young (2010) Uses and gratifications of social media: A comparison of Facebook and instant messaging, *Bulletin of Science, Technology & Society*, 30(5), pp 350–361; B. Gülnar, Ş. Balci and V. Çakir (2010) Motivations of Facebook, YouTube and similar website users, *Bilig*, 54, pp 161–184; N. Park, K.F. Kee, and S. Valenzuela (2009) Being immersed in social networking environment: Facebook groups, uses and gratifications, and social outcomes, *CyberPsychology Behavior*, 12, pp 729–733; C.M.K. Cheung and M.K.O.

Lee (2009) Understanding the sustainability of a virtual community: Model development and empirical test, *Journal of Information Science*, 35(3), pp 279–298.

Chapter 6

[1] Know Your Meme (2020) See? Nobody cares, *Know Your Meme* [online]. Available at: https://knowyourmeme.com/memes/see-nobody-cares [Accessed 8 December 2022].

[2] *Jurassic Park* (1993) [Film] Universal Pictures Ambling Entertainment.

[3] M. Crichton (2012) *Jurassic Park*, New York: Ballantine Books.

[4] In conversations with interview participants the perception of internet research as possibly predatory was raised by two participants.

[5] P. Kollock and M. Smith (1996) Managing the virtual commons: Cooperation and conflict in computer communities, in S. Herring (ed) *Computer Mediated Communication*, Amsterdam: John Benjamins, pp 109–128.

[6] Katz is the first to be credited in print with taking on the question of lurkers and his phrase 'luring the lurkers' is repeatedly cited or utilized in lurking research. Within creator communities there are several channels devoted to how to lure the lurkers for page views. For example, see *Luring the Lurkers (1/3) – SanniHalla* [online]. Available at: https://twitchstats.net/clip/AbrasiveBlueEndiveKappaPride-YRstwXrbk6-9m9ne [Accessed 7 December 2022].

[7] I am using the word capture as it is the standard term in the social sciences for data collection. However, I wish to note that I do so fully aware of the colonial context in which this word can also be understood.

[8] M. Binder (2020) Twitter tests asking if you actually want to read an article before retweeting it, *Mashable* [online]. Available at: https://mashable.com/article/twitter-asks-if-you-want-to-read-before-retweet [Accessed 7 December 2022].

[9] This says nothing of whether or not one might have read the article on another platform or through an off-platform digital subscription or even, in an offline print version.

[10] B. Miller and C. O'Donnell (2013) Opening a window into reading development: Eye movements' role within a broader literacy research framework, *School Psychology Review*, 42(2), pp 123–139. Available at: https://www.ncbi.nlm.nih.gov/pmc/articles/PMC3875 174/ [Accessed 30 December 2019].

[11] Although Javal is often credited with being the first one to measure eye movements, he did not measure, but rather observed, the reading process. See N.J. Wade and B.W. Tatler (2009) Did Javal measure eye movements during reading? *Journal of Eye Movement Research*, 2(5).

[12] N.J. Wade (2015) How were eye movements recorded before Yarbus? *Perception*, 44(8–9), pp 851–883.

[13] This technique was so painful for participants that they needed to have cocaine administered as a desensitizing agent in order to participate in the study. See M. Mikac (2022) The history behind eye tracking, *EyeLogic* [online] 2 March. Available at: https://www.eyelogicsolutions.com/history-behind-eye-tracking/ [Accessed 8 December 2022].

[14] L. Itti and C. Koch (2001) Computational modelling of visual attention, *Nature Reviews Neuroscience*, 2(3), pp 194–203; and Z. Bylinskii, N.W. Kim, P. O'Donovan, S. Alsheikh, S. Madan, H. Pfister, F. Durand, B. Russell, and A. Hertzmann (2017) Learning visual importance for graphic designs and data visualizations, *Proceedings of the 30th Annual ACM Symposium on User Interface Software and Technology*. doi:10.1145/3126594.3126653; J. Nielsen and K. Pernice (2010) *Eyetracking Web Usability*, New York: New Riders.

[15] K. Rayner (1998) Eye movements in reading and information processing: 20 years of research, *Psychological Bulletin*, 124(3), pp 372–422.

16 G.W. McConkie and K. Rayner (1975) The span of the effective stimulus during a fixation in reading, *Perception & Psychophysics*, 17(6), pp 578–586; and K. Rayner (1986) Eye movements and the perceptual span in beginning and skilled readers, *Journal of Experimental Child Psychology*, 41(2), pp 211–236; and K. Rayner and J. Bertera (1979) Reading without a fovea, *Science*, 206(4417), pp 468–469.

17 A.W. Inhoff and K. Rayner (1986) Parafoveal word processing during eye fixations in reading: Effects of word frequency, *Perception & Psychophysics*, 40(6), pp 431–439; and K. Rayner (1986) Eye movements and the perceptual span in beginning and skilled readers, *Journal of Experimental Child Psychology*, 41(2), pp 211–236.

18 N. Valliappan, N. Dai, E. Steinberg, J. He, K. Rogers, V. Ramachandran, P. Xu, M. Shojaeizadeh, L. Guo, K. Kohlhoff, and V. Navalpakkam (2020) Accelerating eye movement research via accurate and affordable smartphone eye tracking, *Nature Communications*, 11(1), p 4553.

19 See N. Ellison, P. Triệu, S. Schoenebeck, R. Brewer, and A. Israni (2020) Why we don't click: Interrogating the relationship between viewing and clicking in social media contexts by exploring the 'non-click', *Journal of Computer-Mediated Communication*, 25(6).

For Takahashi et al, they write that 'lurkers can have one of the following roles: The "active lurker as propagator", who propagates information or knowledge gained from an online community to others outside it; The "active lurker as practitioner" who uses such information or knowledge in their own or organizational activities. The "active lurker candidate" where the online community affects the lurker's thought; The "persistent lurker" where the online community does not affect the lurker's thought.' See M. Takahashi, M. Fujimoto, and N. Yamasaki (2003) The active lurker, *ACM SIGGROUP Bulletin*, 24(1).

20 See B.K. AlShebli, T. Rahwan, and W.L. Woon (2018) The preeminence of ethnic diversity in scientific collaboration, *Nature Communications*, 9(1); and K. Powell (2018) These labs are remarkably diverse: Here's why they're winning at science, *Nature*, 558(7708), pp 19–22.

21 See J. Mcneil (2021) *Lurking: How a Person Became a User*, s.l.: Picador.

22 A robust bibliographic overview of the field of lurking research can be found in N. Sun, P.P.L. Rau, and L. Ma (2014) Understanding lurkers in online communities: A literature review, *Computers in Human Behavior*, 38, pp 100–117. Some specific articles and papers that I found particularly useful in understanding how to recruit people to patriciate in a study on lurking include S. Honeychurch, A. Bozkurt, L. Singh, and A. Koutropoulos (2017) Learners on the periphery: Lurkers as invisible learners, *European Journal of Open, Distance and E-Learning*, 21(1), pp 192–211; N. Edelmann, R. Krimmer, and P. Parycek (2017) How online lurking contributes value to e-participation: A conceptual approach to evaluating the role of lurkers in e-participation, *Fourth International Conference on eDemocracy & eGovernment (ICEDEG) IEEE*, Quito, Ecuador, pp 86–93; B. Nonnecke and J. Preece (2001) Why lurkers lurk, in paper presented at the Americas conference on information systems conference, Boston. Available at: http://www.cis.uoguelph.ca/~nonnecke/resea rch/whylurk.pdf [Accessed 6 November 2023]; B. Nonnecke and J. Preece (2003) Silent participants: Getting to know lurkers better, in C. Lueg and D. Fisher (eds) *From Usenet to CoWebs: Interacting with Social Information Spaces*, New York: Springer, pp 110–132; B. Nonnecke, J. Preece, D. Andrews, and B. Voutour (2004) Online lurkers tell why they lurk, in paper presented at the 10th Americas conference on information systems, New York. Available at: http://www.cis.uoguelph.ca/~nonnecke/research/OnlineLur kersTellWhy.pdf [Accessed 6 November 2023]; M. Popovac and C. Fullwood (2019) The psychology of online lurking, in A. Attrill-Smith, C. Fullwood, M. Keep, and D.J. Kuss (eds) *The Oxford Handbook of Cyberpsychology*, Oxford: Oxford University Press, pp 285–305.

23 R. Calixte, A. Rivera, O. Oridota, W. Beauchamp, and M. Camacho-Rivera (2020) Social and demographic patterns of health-related internet use among adults in the United States: A secondary data analysis of the health information national trends survey, *International Journal of Environmental Research and Public Health*, 17(18), p 6856.

24 See A. Park and M. Conway (2018) Tracking health related discussions on Reddit for public health applications, *AMIA Annual Symposium Proceedings*, [online], pp 1362–1371. Available at: https://www.ncbi.nlm.nih.gov/pmc/articles/PMC5977623/ [Accessed 8 December 2022].

25 E. Sikkens, M.V. San, S. Sieckelinck, H. Boeije, and M.D. Winter (2016) Participant recruitment through social media: Lessons learned from a qualitative radicalization study using Facebook, *Field Methods*, 29(2), pp 130–139.

26 E. Sikkens, M.V. San, S. Sieckelinck, H. Boeije and M.D. Winter (2016) Participant recruitment through social media: Lessons learned from a qualitative radicalization study using Facebook, *Field Methods*, 29(2), pp 130–139.

27 E. Sikkens, M.V. San, S. Sieckelinck, H. Boeije and M.D. Winter (2016) Participant recruitment through social media: Lessons learned from a qualitative radicalization study using Facebook, *Field Methods*, 29(2), pp 130–139.

28 J.T. Child and S.C. Starcher (2016) Fuzzy Facebook privacy boundaries: Exploring mediated lurking, vague-booking, and Facebook privacy management, *Computers in Human Behavior*, 54, 483–490.

29 The Association of Internet Researchers has multiple editions of its guide for ethical research. The second edition is most helpful in terms of lurking scholarship. See A. Markham (2012) *Ethical Decision-Making and Internet Research: Recommendations from the AoIR Ethics Working Committee (Version 2.0)*, Association of Internet Researchers [online]. Available at: https://aoir.org/reports/ethics2.pdf [Accessed 7 December 2022].

30 See the joint international briefing provided by Full Fact, Africa Check, and Chequeado at Full Fact.org (2020) Who is most likely to believe and to share misinformation? [online]. Available at: https://fullfact.org/media/uploads/who-believes-shares-misinformation.pdf [Accessed 7 December 2022].

31 The Knight Foundation, the philanthropic organization of American journalism magnates and brothers John S. and James L. Knight, offers over 300 grants per year for 'innovative ideas that advance informed communities'. In 2021, the most recent year for which funding information was available, the Knight Foundation funded 358 grants to the tune of US$3.89 billion dollars. See Knight Foundation (2021) *Assets and Grantmaking*, Knight Foundation [online]. Available at: https://knightfoundation. org/about/financial-info/ [Accessed 10 January 2023]. In 2015 they were also earlier financiers of what come to be known as CrowdTangle. See S. Kessler (2015) The secret tool that Upworthy, BuzzFeed, and everyone else is using to win Facebook, *Fast Company* [online]. Available at: https://www.fastcompany.com/3040951/the-secret-tool-that-upworthy-buzzfeed-and-everyone-else-is-using-to-win-facebook [Accessed 7 December 2022].

32 R. Brooks (2011) The Occupy Network winning the internet, *Netroots Foundation* [online]. Available at: https://www.netrootsfoundation.org/2011/11/the-occupy-netw ork/ [Accessed 8 December 2022].

33 B. Silverman (2019) CrowdTangle for academics and researchers [online]. Available at: https://www.facebook.com/formedia/blog/CrowdTangle-for-academics-and-rese archers [Accessed 7 December 2022].

34 B. Silverman (2019) CrowdTangle for academics and researchers [online]. Available at: https://www.facebook.com/formedia/blog/CrowdTangle-for-academics-and-rese archers [Accessed 7 December 2022].

35 K. Roose and F. Giglietto (nd) Facebook's top 10, *Twitter* [online]. Available at: https://twitter.com/FacebooksTop10?ref_src=twsrc%5Etfw%7Ctwcamp%5Etwe etembed%7Ctwterm%5E1402319409343909889%7Ctwgr%5E889d94280b8e830a1 6111dc6bc62ae18f1f9d486%7Ctwcon%5Es1_&ref_url=https%3A%2F%2Fwww.nyti mes.com%2F2021%2F07%2F14%2Ftechnology%2Ffacebook-data.html [Accessed 7 December 2022].

36 K. Roose and F. Giglietto (nd) Facebook's top 10, *Twitter* [online]. Available at: https://twitter.com/FacebooksTop10?ref_src=twsrc%5Etfw%7Ctwcamp%5Etweetembed%7Ctwt erm%5E1402319409343909889%7Ctwgr%5E889d94280b8e830a16111dc6bc62a e18f1f9d486%7Ctwcon%5Es1_&ref_url=https%3A%2F%2Fwww.nytimes.com%2F2 021%2F07%2F14%2Ftechnology%2Ffacebook-data.html [Accessed 7 December 2022].

37 K. Roose (2021) Inside Facebook's data wars, *The New York Times* [online] 14 July. Available at: https://www.nytimes.com/2021/07/14/technology/facebook-data.html [Accessed 7 December 2022].

38 A. Thompson (2020) Why the right wing has a massive advantage on Facebook, *Politico* [online]. Available at: https://www.politico.com/news/2020/09/26/facebook-conser vatives-2020-421146 [Accessed 7 December 2022].

39 K. Roose (2021) Inside Facebook's data wars, *The New York Times* [online] 14 July. Available at: https://www.nytimes.com/2021/07/14/technology/facebook-data.html [Accessed 7 December 2022].

40 M. Allen and D. Nather (2020) Zuckerberg: It's 'just wrong' to consider Facebook a right-wing echo chamber, *Axios* [online]. Available at: https://www.axios.com/2020/ 09/09/zuckerberg-facebook-conservatives-algorithm [Accessed 7 December 2022].

41 See A. Bogle (2022) One of the biggest tools for analysing Facebook is being shut down – by Facebook, *ABC News* [online] 15 August. Available at: https://www.abc.net.au/news/ science/2022-08-16/facebook-CrowdTangle-meta-disinformation-transparency/101325 544 [Accessed 7 December 2022].

42 D. Alba (2022) Meta pulls support for tool used to keep misinformation in check, *Bloomberg.com*, [online] 23 June. Available at: https://www.bloomberg.com/news/artic les/2022-06-23/meta-pulls-support-for-tool-used-to-keep-misinformation-in-check [Accessed 7 December 2022].

43 T. Shane (2021) What Facebook gutting CrowdTangle means for misinformation, *First Draft* [online]. Available at: https://firstdraftnews.org/articles/%E2%80%A8what-faceb ook-gutting-crowdtangle-means-for-misinformation/ [Accessed 7 December 2022].

44 J. Cox (2019) Facebook quietly changes search tool used by investigators, abused by companies, *Vice* [online]. Available at: https://www.vice.com/en/article/zmpgmx/faceb ook-stops-graph-search [Accessed 7 December 2022].

45 T. Scott (2013) Actual Facebook graph searches [online]. Available at: https://actualfa cebookgraphsearches.tumblr.com [Accessed 6 November 2023].

46 T. Shane (2021) What Facebook gutting CrowdTangle means for misinformation, *First Draft* [online]. Available at: https://firstdraftnews.org/articles/%E2%80%A8what-faceb ook-gutting-crowdtangle-means-for-misinformation/ [Accessed 7 December 2022].

Conclusion

1 In a discussion with Jenkins and Itō (2016), danah boyd questions the current emphasis on active participation as a more valuable contribution than passive participation. She asks, 'What does it mean to always focus on active participation, regardless of the quality of that contribution?' (p 112). boyd posits these two salient questions: 'Can someone be a valuable and participatory lurker?' and 'What does high quality listening look like?' (p 112). The discussion among the scholars in this text does not extend into imagining

what this might look like. Reading this question is what, in part, prompted me to further explore the possibilities. See H. Jenkins, M. Ito, and d. boyd (2017) *Participatory Culture in a Networked Era: A Conversation on Youth, Learning, Commerce, and Politics*, Cambridge: Polity.

2   For more information on ecoliteracy and the polluted and toxic nature of digital information exchange, see W. Phillips and R.M. Milner (2021) *You Are Here: A Field Guide for Navigating Polluted Information*, Cambridge, MA: MIT Press.

3   I am using the term second definition in a purely connotative sense. The *Oxford English Dictionary*, which organizes definitions by prevalent print usage, determines that the primary definition for the adjective valuable is 'importance', with 'worth a lot of money' placed in the secondary position.

4   K. Swisher (2021) If you were on Parler, you saw the mob coming, *The New York Times* [online] 7 January. Available at: https://www.nytimes.com/2021/01/07/opinion/sway-kara-swisher-john-matze.html [Accessed 7 December 2022].

5   Statista (2022) Facebook users worldwide 2020, *Statista* [online]. Available at: https://www.statista.com/statistics/264810/number-of-monthly-active-facebook-users-worldwide/ [Accessed 7 December 2022].

6   N. Srnicek (2017) *Platform Capitalism*, Cambridge: Polity.

7   A. Robertson (2021) Facebook employee warned it used 'deeply wrong' ad metrics to boost revenue, *The Verge* [online]. Available at: https://www.theverge.com/2021/2/18/22289232/facebook-ad-revenue-proposed-reach-inflation-lawsuit-unredacted-filings [Accessed 7 December 2022]; and C. Welch (2018) Facebook may have knowingly inflated its video metrics for over a year, *The Verge* [online]. Available at: https://www.theverge.com/2018/10/17/17989712/facebook-inaccurate-video-metrics-inflation-lawsuit [Accessed 7 December 2022]; and R. Todd (2018) Advertiser class action claims Facebook over estimates audience size, *The Recorder*. Available at: https://www.reuters.com/business/facebook-advertisers-can-pursue-class-action-over-ad-rates-2022-03-29/#:~:text=The%20lawsuit%20began%20in%202018,high%20premiums%20for%20ad%20placements [Accessed 6 November 2023].

8   D. Meacham (2022) There are an estimated 30 million dead people on Facebook, *PopCrush* [online]. Available at: https://popcrush.com/facebook-30-million-dead-users-data/ [Accessed 7 December 2022].

9   See C.J. Öhman and D. Watson (2019) Are the dead taking over Facebook? A Big Data approach to the future of death online, *Big Data & Society*, 6(1).

10 See N. Forbes (2020) Lurkers are us: When nothing signifies something, *Debating Communities and Networks 11* [online]. Available at: https://networkconference.net studies.org/2020OUA/2020/04/26/lurkers-are-us-when-nothing-signifies-something/ [Accessed 7 December 2022]; and H. Krasnova, H. Wenninger, T. Widjaja, and P. Buxmann (2013) Envy on Facebook: A hidden threat to users' life satisfaction? In *11th International Conference on Wirtschaftsinformatik (WI), Leipzig, Germany*; and S. Kushner (2016) Read only: The persistence of lurking in Web 2.0, *First Monday*, 21(6).

11 Kollock and Smith penned the original analysis, stating that lurkers were selfish free-riders. See P. Kollock and M. Smith (1996) Managing the virtual commons: Cooperation and conflict in computer communities, in S.C. Herring (ed) *Computer Mediated Communication: Linguistic, Social, and Cross-Cultural Perspectives*, Amsterdam: John Benjamins, pp 109–128 and Chapter 1 for more information on why that proposition was later found to be unsound.

12 Twitter (2001) 3 June "Reader Mode" [online]. Available at: https://twitter.com/premium/status/1400452694649696265 [Accessed 14 August 2023].

13 In its initial 2021 rollout, the price point was US$2.99 for iOS subscribers. See I. Mehta (2022) "Twitter is increasing the price of Twitter Blue from $2.99 to $4.99

per month. *TechCrunch* [online]. Available at: https://techcrunch.com/2022/07/28/twitter-is-increasing-the-price-of-twitter-blue-from-2-99-to-4-99-per-month/?guc counter=1&guce_referrer=aHR0cHM6Ly93d3cuZ29vZ2xlLmNvbS8&guce_refer rer_sig=AQAAAAK-aAsbLkpIL07n52AVcuE5_5MIF3WEV37kGY5yuS9z4MPmSY z3qc_wM-SNacvnvMe14k1915pQ4PM1e6-3F_XvUzClaNnPKqyg9cwjNhryR5I qM1lX8NGWe2fUNor94ScmbFMFI5muBjTl7UvkFlORSNq136YkPPFBukzNX cRG [Accessed 14 August 2023]; and I. Mehta (2023) Twitter Blue is now available on Android at the same price as iOS, *TechCrunch* [online]. Available at: https://techcru nch.com/2023/01/18/twitter-blue-is-now-available-on-android-at-the-same-price-as-ios/ [Accessed 14 August 2023]. A more comprehensive list of pricing by geographic location and tier can be found: X (2023). *About X Premium.* [online] help.twitter.com. Available at: https://help.twitter.com/en/using-x/x-premium#tbpricing-bycountry [Accessed 5 November 2023].

14   J. Shapero (2023) Twitter limits how many tweets users can see a day, *The Hill* [online]. Available at: https://thehill.com/policy/technology/4077620-twitter-limits-how-many-tweets-users-can-see-a-day/ [Accessed 14 August 2023].

15   See help.twitch.tv (nd) Customer support [online]. Available at: https://help.twitch.tv/s/article/twitch-affiliate-program-faq?language=en_US [Accessed 7 December 2022].

16   Streaming Auntie (2022) Interview with Streaming Auntie @itsmadqueen, 21 July, Zoom.

17   See Twitchstats (2022) *Luring the Lurkers (1/3) – SanniHalla* [online]. Available at: https://twitchstats.net/clip/AbrasiveBlueEndiveKappaPride-YRstwXrbk6-9m9ne [Accessed 7 December 2022].

18   See J. Williams, R. Heiser, and S.J. Chinn (2012) Social media posters and lurkers: The impact on team identification and game attendance in minor league baseball, *Journal of Direct, Data and Digital Marketing Practice*, 13(4), pp 295–310.

19   For 2022 pricing, see N. Fulmer (2022) Comparing beer, hot dog, and ticket prices at Major League Baseball parks, *WebstaurantStore* [online]. Available at: https://www.webst aurantstore.com/blog/628/beer-hot-dog-and-ticket-prices-at-major-league-baseball-parks.html [Accessed 7 December 2022].

20   See T. Spangler (2019) Facebook to pay $40 million to settle claims it inflated video viewing data, *Variety* [online]. Available at: https://variety.com/2019/digital/news/facebook-settlement-video-advertising-lawsuit-40-million-1203361133/ [Accessed 10 January 2023]; and J. Stempel (2022) Meta's Facebook to pay $90 million to settle privacy lawsuit over user tracking, *Reuters* [online] 15 February. Available at: https://www.reuters.com/technology/metas-facebook-pay-90-million-settle-privacy-lawsuit-over-user-track ing-2022-02-15/ [Accessed 6 November 2023].

21   Refreshments is defined as one hot dog and two beers per person by N. Fulmer (2022) Comparing beer, hot dog, and ticket prices at Major League Baseball parks, *WebstaurantStore* [online]. Available at: https://www.webstaurantstore.com/blog/628/beer-hot-dog-and-ticket-prices-at-major-league-baseball-parks.html [Accessed 7 December 2022].

22   See S. Perez (2022) Facebook is losing its grip as a 'Top 10' app as BeReal and TikTok grow, *TechCrunch* [online]. Available at: https://techcrunch.com/2022/08/18/facebook-is-los ing-its-grip-as-a-top-10-app-as-bereal-and-tiktok-grow/ [Accessed 7 December 2022].

23   See M. Whitehead (2020) Why people leave Facebook – and what it tells us about the future of social media, *The Conversation* [online]. Available at: https://theconversation.com/why-people-leave-facebook-and-what-it-tells-us-about-the-future-of-social-media-128952 [Accessed 7 December 2022]; and A. Perrin (2018) Americans are changing their relationship with Facebook, *Pew Research Center* [online]. Available at: https://www.pewr esearch.org/fact-tank/2018/09/05/americans-are-changing-their-relationship-with-faceb ook/ [Accessed 7 December 2022].

Index

References to figures and photographs appear in *italic* type; those in **bold** type refer to tables. References to endnotes show both the page number and the note number (231n3).